Proclaim His Word

Volume III:

Joseph Fichtner, O.S.C.

Proclaim His Word

Homiletic Themes

for

Sundays and Holydays

CYCLE B

ALBA · HOUSE   NEW · YORK

SOCIETY OF ST. PAUL, 2187 VICTORY BLVD., STATEN ISLAND, NEW YORK 10314

Library of Congress Cataloging in Publication Data

Fichtner, Joseph.
    Proclaim His word.

    CONTENTS: v. 1.   Cycle C.—v. 2.
Cycle A.—v. 3.
Cycle B.
    1.   Church year sermons.
    2.   Catholic Church—
Sermons. 3. Sermons, American. I. Title.
BX1756.   F46P76   252   73-5726
ISBN   0-8189-0273-6

Nihil Obstat:
James T. O'Connor, S.T.D.
Censor Librorum

Imprimatur:
+ James P. Mahoney, D.D.
Vicar General, Archdiocese of New York
May 29, 1975

*Designed, printed and bound in the United States of
America by the Fathers and Brothers of the Society of St. Paul,
2187 Victory Boulevard, Staten Island, New York, 10314,
as part of their communications apostolate.*

1 2 3 4 5 6 7 8 9 (Current Printing: first digit).

To

Father Michael J. Vecchio

Maggie, Irene, and

friends and parishioners at Madonna,

with sincere thanks

CONTENTS

Foreword

With the publication of this volume (Volume III: Cycle B), this homily series comes to an end. The composition of the homilies that lasted over several years, not counting the remote preparation, was a labor of study, reflection, and prayer. The author hoped that the three volumes would lend help to priests and others who felt the priority of preaching over teaching as restored by Vatican II in its document *Lumen gentium*. He is very grateful to those who have found the homilies helpful and expressed their appreciation to him.

Printed homilies and homily outlines, far from keeping ministers of the word from preparing their own, or relieving them of this duty, can be a powerful aid to better evangelization. If this were not the case, a vast amount of Christian literature dating back to the patristic homilies, and including fragments of Holy Scripture, would have to be discarded or left in oblivion. Homiletic sources have a perennial value, as much as if not more than references for teaching sacred doctrine. Preaching and teaching are distinct forms of proclamation, each having resources of its own in order to accomplish distinct purposes.

Preacher and listener are partners in the dialogue of God's word. The relationship within which God's word is spoken (or written) to and enacted among men is covenantal. It combines call and response, following a dialogic pattern in which one priest can respond to the call of another.

The primary effect of preaching is faith, though not taking place *ex opere operato,* for faith is born of the hearing (and why not reading?) of God's word.

God's word signifies and contains the grace which leads to salvation. It charms every man with an open mind, a generous heart, and a good will. Its appeal to every man is an enlightenment to his mind and an encouragement to his will, but more than that it engages his whole personality. Such was the purpose behind the following homilies.

Joseph Fichtner, O.S.C.
Duquesne University
Pittsburgh, Pa.

ADVENT SEASON

First Sunday of Advent
Is 63:16-17, 19; 64:2-7; 1 Cor 1:3-9; Mk 13:33-37

Father and Son

Our neighborhood has a teenage boy, a widow's son, who is beginning to cause trouble and becoming a nuisance. At times he's surly, loud-mouthed, back-talking, self-centered. As the oldest of five children, this boy needs a father. The widowed mother, while trying her best to raise her children into good, decent Christians, has more than she can handle. The boy needs the discipline, firmness, guidance, and example a father can give him. He's just at that age when fatherhood can be so meaningful and helpful to him.

1. The Fatherhood of God

The experience of this fatherless boy is similar to what the human experience would be without the fatherhood of God. Thanks be to God, he has never left us fatherless. The Judaic-Christian belief in the fatherhood of God is one of our oldest traditions. The psalmist in the Isaian reading is addressing God, "You are our Father." God is our Father not merely by creating us but by redeeming us, his people, and imparting to us a life that shares in his love. Under the Old Covenant with him, the Jewish nation felt the love, care and concern of God particularly at the time he liberated it from Egyptian slavery. The head of the Jewish family was the father-ruler, therefore

their family life was patriarchal. The intimacy of a father
within the family was carried over into their belief in
the one God. The immediacy or nearness of God was
expressed in the name "Father." All Jewish prayers were
directed to God the Father.

What a difference it would make in the life of our
neighbor boy could he feel the immediate relationship
of a father. He has had to go through life till now without
ever calling anyone "father" or "dad." Pray as he might
to God the Father, his prayer will lack the fatherly support only a human father can give him.

Now, although the Hebrew people never lacked God's
tender protection and loving support, because God always
proved himself faithful, the Hebrew psalmist prayed for
a theophany more wonderful than Sinai. On Mt. Sinai
God favored Moses with his extraordinary presence. Still
the people looked for a special sign of the divine favor.
We act as they when we pray God to bless America in a
special way, to stand beside her and guide her.

2. Sonship

God did grant the Hebrew request by sending us his
Son. God's presence in Jesus is far more extraordinary
than his presence on Mt. Sinai. The fatherhood of God
was further ennobled by Jesus' sonship. A new relationship was established the moment Jesus became the Son
of Mary. We are all sons of God, as the Hebrew people
believed, but never so much so as when Jesus became our
brother. What the fatherhood of God lacked in the Old
Testament was the brotherhood of Jesus. Through a sonship shared with him we're brothers of one another and
sons of God.

St. Paul starts his first letter to the Corinthians with
a thanksgiving prayer to God the Father. A Hebrew by
birth and brought up in a strong Hebrew tradition, he's
thankful for the grace and peace that come from "God

our Father." Yet, because he's a convert Christian, he knows grace and peace don't come from the Father alone. They're mediated by Jesus, the Son of God. The Father "has joined you to his Son." Together they're the actors in the salvation of mankind.

Paul maintains that God "will keep you steady and without blame until the last day." Grace and peace do keep you steady and without blame. Don't forget, they're gifts coming to you from the Father-Son duo. Appreciate them gratefully, and you will see they're a participation in God's own fidelity to his people.

In our need for Fatherhood we're no different from the unruly neighbor boy. What happens to us if we break away from the fatherhood of God and the brotherhood of Jesus? We turn rebellious and hard-hearted. Our hearts bleed for the poor boy who has to shift more or less for himself, fatherless. But we're to be pitied the more who try to spend life outside Jesus' unity with the Father. Jesus dedicated his life to the Father; we should do no less.

3. A third theophany

Later in the same letter (1 Cor 10:16-17), Paul points out where we can find Jesus and join his company—in the Eucharist, which is an act of thanksgiving in itself. "The blessing-cup that we bless is a communion with the blood of Christ, and the bread that we break is a communion with the body of Christ." One loaf, one body, many as we are. Jesus in the Eucharistic meal isn't Father-less. God's presence is to be found there as on Mt. Sinai and in Jesus himself. When Paul sat down to a Eucharistic meal with the Corinthians, he and they were in good company. The same is true of our participation in the Eucharist. Father and Son bestow grace and peace upon us there. They keep us steady and irreproachable until "the day of our Lord Jesus Christ." The Eucharist prepares us for it.

4. At home with God

As the Hebrews of old prayed for a theophany greater than that of Mt. Sinai, so should we pray for the final appearance of Jesus Christ. We'll find our future in God. God the Father is our beginning and end. God's Son is our brother. Through and in and with him, we praise, love, and return to the Father.

Man doesn't experience the full spiritual and universal fatherhood of God until he arrives in his heavenly home. His life on this earth is a waiting-for the day when Jesus will reveal himself again, and not only himself but the Father too. Meanwhile man doesn't have the potential to be a fully grown son of God. He remains weak and unsteady and blameworthy till the "master of the house" takes him in hand. Thankfully, man is to be a son of God in the Father's house forever.

Solemnity of the Immaculate Conception
Gn 3:9-15, 20; Ep 1:3-6, 11-12; Lk 1:26-38

Mary and the People of God

1. Mother of the living

Readings one and three describe two of the most momentous occasions in the history of mankind. If they were to be set in newsprint, they would have to make the headlines, the exclusive stories of human downfall and human salvation. The one involves Eve, "the mother of all those who live," the other Mary, the mother of all those who are saved, of the redeemed.

As far apart as the two occasions and the two women are in time, historically, they're nonetheless interconnected in divine plan and meaning. Looking back on the first occasion, the scene in the garden, we see that already then God didn't leave man in his sinfulness but promised him a way out of it. The promise of salvation is hidden in the words: "It will crush your head and you will strike its heel." Church art represents this truth in its use of the statue of Mary standing atop the planet earth, with the snake or serpent under her feet. The serpent is symbolic of evil, but the evil one has no power over her.

You may wonder how Mary the Mother of God figures in the first occasion, since the English text speaks of an "it." Is she "it"? To make a long story short, the original Hebrew text has the pronoun "it," referring to the offspring which is Christ the Lord. He is the one who wins the victory over satan, sin, and death. The Greek translators by some miscue changed the "it" into a "he," namely, Christ the Redeemer Lord. But the Latin Vulgate edition of the Bible rendered the pronoun "she" and began a long-standing tradition in the Church which applied the text to Mary.

2. The single, sinless one

Whatever you may think of this confusion, the point that matters is that Mary was kept free from original sin by the redeeming power of her Son. Adam and Eve, like Mary, came into existence without the taint of original sin, then they originated it. Mary was the single one in all of human history after them to be favored by God with freedom from original sin. Catholic faith holds too that Mary in no way contributed to original sin with sins of her own. She remained sinless. We can't make such a claim for ourselves. We can't guarantee that we wouldn't originate sin if the human record were clear, nor can we deny how much our own sins have added to original sin. The sins of our world have aggravated original sin. They have ratified or approved of original sin.

3. Favoured by God

What Paul has to say in his letter to the Ephesians about the people of God has special application to Mary. She was unique among "the people who would put their hopes in Christ before he came." Her intention as far as we know was to be married but childless; she pledged her virginity to God so as to be totally dedicated to him. Other women who before her were counted among the people of God were childless for a while—Sarah, Rebekah, Samson's mother, and Hannah, but none was so favored as she to be virgin and Mother of God.

One day in class a student asked why God chose the Hebrew people to be his very own—why did he single them out? This student expressed the question implied in the verse: "How odd / Of God / To choose / The Jews." We read an answer in Deuteronomy: "If Yahweh set his heart on you and chose you (Israel), it was not because you outnumbered other peoples: you were the least of all peoples. It was for love of you. . . " (7:7f.). We simply can't fathom the mystery of his love, neither in choosing Israel nor in choosing one of their own to be the Mother of his Son. Mary was none other than a simple maiden from the unpretentious town of Nazareth.

Mary was chosen just as the people of God "in Christ, to be holy and spotless, and to live through love in his presence." Even though his divine love stumps us with its mystery, Christ is human enough in his love to expect some response from his people in the form of either attracting or repaying or reciprocating his love. Mary, called "favoured" by the angel who brings a message from God, calls herself the "handmaid" or slave of God. She lets his will be done to her. God loves those especially who accept and do his will. So did Jesus in the garden of Gethsemane let the divine will be done to him (Lk 22:42). And so must we be humbly obedient to his will as we pray in the Our Father, "your will be done" (Mt 6:10).

4. An Eve-Mary parallel

The two readings from Genesis and Luke are marked with sharp and clear contrasts. The first news about human sinning is drowned out by the first news of human saving. Discovering herself to be naked, Eve feels ashamed of her sin and tries to hide herself from God. Mary too is afraid but for another reason, and is reassured by the angel that she has won "God's favour." The first woman in the story of mankind is enchanted by a serpent, while the first woman in Christianity is addressed by an angel.

The strongest contrast between the two is to be noted in their reactions to their separate situations. In the disastrous situation of original sin the entire blame sometimes falls upon Eve. Adam blames her and God for giving her to him, but Eve shifts the blame upon the serpent. How characteristically human she is in not pleading guilty, in refusing to take the rap.

5. Cause for praise and thanks

The Church through the ages hails Mary as specially blessed by God. She is "to make us praise the glory of his grace, his free gift to us in the Beloved." Together with her Son she is sufficient cause for us to praise God for all time and eternity. Of what practical benefit to us is the annual succession of liturgies in her honor? How relevant is her singular privilege of the immaculate conception? What has it to do with our relationship to God and to Christ?

In a time when human dignity, not to speak of divine majesty, suffers, nothing could be more pragmatic for us than to give praise to God for such a creature as Mary. Sinful and unworthy as we are, we have deserved through Mary to receive the Creator and Redeemer of our life, and therefore we ought always to sing praise and thanksgiving to God.

The solemnity of the immaculate conception is itself an occasion for us, the people of God, to recall our origins in Eve and Mary, and to praise and thank God for the Woman who prays for us sinners now and at the hour of our death.

Second Sunday of Advent
Is 40:1-5, 9-11; 2 P 3:8-14; Mk 1:1-8

Baptism of Repentance

1. Repent and be baptized? Hardly.

He didn't mean it as such, but the gospel-writer Mark was guilty of a pious exaggeration in saying that "all Judaea and all the people of Jerusalem made their way" to John the Baptist. Not everybody went running to him, nor did everybody submit to his baptism. I'm thinking of the Judaean governor Pontius Pilate and the high priests Annas and Caiaphas.

Why didn't they repent and ask John for his baptism? Was it because they weren't in need of it? That could hardly be the reason.

Pontius Pilate was reported to be a man "naturally inflexible, a blend of self-will and relentlessness." With such character traits, he wasn't about to knuckle under for his subjects, least of all for John the Baptist, the desert reformer. Governors customarily stored the sacred vestments for use in the temple, but Pilate had no regard for the sacredness of Jerusalem. He took money from the temple treasury to defray the building cost of an aqueduct. His people were doubly taxed, paying government revenue and temple dues.

Annas and his son-in-law Caiaphas were the honored religious leaders of the time, "pre-eminent over" their fellowmen (Lv 21:10). The VIPs of the Jewish community, they represented and spoke for the Jewish nation to governor and emperor. Only they could enter the holy of holies. Usually they were members of a wealthy priestly family. Power was concentrated in the hands of a few

rich and influential families. Annas and Caiaphas were
reluctant to let go of it.

2. The political hurdle

Should we rightfully expect people in high places,
powerful political rulers and religious leaders, to repent
and ask for forgiveness? High and mighty officials have
an encouraging line of talk. They describe how rosy things
are or will be under their regime. If things go wrong in
government, they try to smother social criticism, keep a
tight security about themselves, and overpower all resistance. The nature of politics is to cover up its own
mistakes. John the Baptist had to be decapitated for
Herod to save face.

What we've been thinking about historically the prophets Isaiah and John hinted at poetically. Mountains and
hills, they said, were to be leveled, rough and winding
roads flattened and straightened out. Mountains with
their soaring heights symbolized human pride. The ways
into human hearts choked with egotism should be cleared
and opened before God could lead his people to salvation.
John the Baptist was one of the prophets or messengers
who prepared the way. As so many of the Old Testament
prophets before him who lost their lives for Yahweh,
John was expendable for Christ.

In any confrontation with social evils, the sins of a
society, two alternatives are possible for would-be re-
formers. They can revolt or repent. When Pontius Pilate
was governor under emperor Tiberius Caesar and tetrarch
Herod, there were several attempts at revolt. They were
put down at once. Revolt was met with violence. The real
cure for the ills of society was proclaimed by John the
Baptist, "a baptism of repentance for the forgiveness of
sins." The origin of non-violent repentance wasn't Jerusalem, the center of government and religion; no, it was
at the River Jordan, near Jericho.

3. What is repentance?

Unlike revolt, which sometimes spills blood and costs people their lives, repentance is an interior renewal and forgiveness. It starts from within a man, with a realization of sinfulness and a humble submission. Take the example of John the Baptist who practiced what he proclaimed. He cut back on his food and dress, spent a simple, rugged life in the desert. He felt how small he was in the presence of Jesus. His whole life-style was penitential.

The second letter of Peter catches this same penitential spirit but promotes it not in view of the first coming of Christ, as did the Baptist, but of his second coming, "the Day of the Lord," "the Day of God." Here we're comforted with knowing that the Lord has patience with us all, high and low alike, "wanting nobody to be lost and everybody to be brought to change his ways." Repentance is a two-way street to "the new heavens and new earth," having both a negative and a positive side to it. Negatively, we're "to live lives without spot or stain," which means we have to keep uprooting our faults and sins by confessing them. Positively, while we await Christ's coming (either his first or his last), we "should be living holy and saintly lives."

4. Penitential practice

The best way to prepare for the Lord is *inner* preparation, a change of heart and a mending of faults. The essence of John the Baptist's proclamation and baptism isn't something we can forget about because it was supplanted by Christ's own institution of baptism in the Spirit. Jesus originated the forgiveness of sin in the sacrament of baptism; the spirit of forgiveness must be nurtured throughout our lifetime by penitential works. Sins once forgiven have a way of reintroducing themselves into a life, if not actually then by way of memory or guilt feelings. Sins can never be repented for enough.

I've thought some Pentecostals admirable who claimed to have received a baptism in the Spirit. They experienced within them a second, third, or further conversion. In my opinion, the Pentecostal movement augurs well for those members whose hearts were reconverted to Christ, who tightened their belts and entered upon a simpler way of life. They are contemporary John the Baptists who proclaim by their lives "a baptism of repentance for the forgiveness of sins."

Third Sunday of Advent
Is 61:1-2, 10-11; 1 Th 5:16-24; Jn 1:6-8, 19-28

Sanctity, Sign of Salvation

1. The disenchanted

Some young people I meet off and on campus say how disillusioned, disenchanted they are with the Church. They complain the Church doesn't speak out or use its influence against social abuses in our day. These young people can't identify themselves with a false representation of the Church. And up to this point they're right. What they're saying in a roundabout, negative way is that the only Church that appeals to them is a *holy* Church. It has to be a Church *of saints* before they can believe in it.

Their attitude is in agreement with the teaching of the Isaian prophecy regarding Judah and Jerusalem. Prophetic comfort is given the people who are downhearted over their city, Jerusalem. The divine promise of a Messiah and of a messianic people is held out to them: "he has clothed me in the garments of salvation, he has wrapped me in the cloak of integrity." The aim or purpose of Christ for Israel is the same as for the Church— a holy nation, a holy Church. Only the expression differs; the practice of integrity is synonymous with holiness.

2. Holiness in progress

Holiness isn't a static quality, like an indelible purple ink stamp on a package of goods. It's closer to the aim or purpose St. Paul had for his Thessalonians: "May the God of peace make you perfect and holy." When writing to the Thessalonians he envisioned them moving ever nearer to the goal of the Christian life, holiness. They were to become holier in expectation of their encounter with the risen and returning Christ. His wish and prayer for them was: "May you all be kept safe and blameless. . . ."

This simple little prayer expresses all we need to know about holiness. Words like "growth" "progress" "increase" describe its inner drive, its vital force. The Christian life has to either move forward or slip backward. The momentum doesn't depend on God or Christ alone. The Lord won't make us perfect and holy or keep us safe and blameless unless we set our hearts upon holiness. The "saintly" people you and I are acquainted with, however easy, natural, and happy their life-style seems to be, have the will to make a straight way for the Lord.

We Christians know what we are today, more or less holy. We don't know precisely what we can become. The pace of holiness quickens the more we're attracted to the presence of the Holy. The holy is not only that which is. Surely the Church is as much saintly as it is sinful. But the holy is also that which ought to be, that which demands practice above all.

How always tempting it is to reply to people who criticize the Church for her sinfulness that they should get busy and do something about it. They can better her condition by contributing their own holiness. All our young people can make this much of a contribution. Never too early to start on the road to holiness; indeed, the earlier the better. The love and concern for their fellowmen, a social ideal they respect, is the means and goal of Christian perfection. A car-sticker on a hot rod read "Love is a four-letter word." Real love is spelled with three or six letters: God or Christ. God makes love grow through Christ. God is the source and Christ the model of love.

3. Saints are for real

The picture of holiness Paul sketches for us is given flesh-and-blood realization in the actual lives of the saints. Despite all the hyperbolic stories about them, saints are *real* people because they're Christlike, for Christ alone fully images God. They're full, solid, genuine, happy men and women. You've probably heard others say or have said it yourself, amused, "Saints are hard to live with." The truth is, saints are our best companions on the way of life. The world, the Church, the community, the family can't survive without them.

The youthful complaint against lack of sanctity in the Church makes more sense in that holiness doesn't grow undercover or go underground. The saint has to stand out, and the holiness of the Church must be witnessed to, perceptible. Perhaps, because we live in an age when the billboard clutters the countryside, when advertisements, neon lights, TV commercials, audio-visual aids are part of our daily life, we expect and demand holiness to have more of a shock or sign-value. Our age more than any other in the Church seems to be impressed by holiness. We're all hero-worshippers.

The saints lead transparent lives. Their love for God and their fellowmen has a luster and splendor about it. Their lives, their actions, their prayers have a secret and irresistible attraction for us. Sets of laws, prohibitions and commands, thoughts of heaven or hell put pressure on us; saints *appeal* to us.

4. Saints on the march

God grant that our young people and all people retain their attraction to holiness. Why? Because it takes just a little holiness to appreciate saints. Christ and John the Baptist have no appeal to those not well-disposed to discover sanctity in them. Holiness is an indication of divine love for men. It becomes known, visible to men who are open to and expect it from others. Strange as it may seem, you and I are looking for the coming of the saints, for the time when our Lord Jesus Christ will come with all his saints.

"Oh, Lord I want to be in that number / When the saints come marching in. / We are trav'ling in the footsteps / Of those who have gone before / But we'll all be reunited on a new and sunlit shore. / Oh, Lord I want to be in that number / When the saints come marching in. / Somedays in this world of trouble / He's the only one we need / But I'm waitin' for that mornin' when the new world is revealed."

Fourth Sunday of Advent
2 S 7:1-5, 8-11, 16; Rm 16:25-27; Lk 1:26-38

A Decision for Christ

Decisions, decisions, decisions. Life is full of them. Do they make any difference in life? You bet they do. Even to postpone them is to make a decision. Events, major and minor, hinge upon them. And yet we can't plan our life like a blueprint. One reason is that we can't shake off our past. Another is that the future is not ours to see. Decisions help us to face the mystery of the future.

1. The Davidic family

Decisions played a big part in the life of the Blessed Virgin Mary too. The annunciation by the angel Gabriel was a call to decision. What led up to this and how she got into it, is our theme for today.

The piece from 2 Samuel reads like a prologue to the annunciation. It projects an ancient promise to build a dynasty upon King David. "Yahweh will make you a House." The Hebrew term for "house" has a twofold meaning. It refers to either a building or a family. King David was determined to build a temple for the Lord, for the Lord lived in a tent while David owned a royal palace. The Lord thought otherwise; he had David in mind for the father of a long ancestral line leading up to the Messiah. This was the first event in the long advent interconnecting David with the Messiah.

Luke, who must have learnt of the annunciation directly from Mary or through others, traces the Davidic family line through Joseph, Mary's husband. Although David is a skeleton in the family closet, Luke makes no excuse for him. Jesus is the Davidic Messiah, and his mother Mary is the real temple, the real house of God. God's glory rests not so much in temple or church buildings as in people. The Jerusalem temple was not to welcome the Messiah into human life. Rather a small nucleus of people (particularly Mary and Joseph) welcomed him.

2. Deeply disturbed

The angelic annunciation to Mary is for us a piece of the Good News. It was for Mary also but not in the same way. It "deeply disturbed" her. You may know this from your own experience, a call from God can be disturbing especially if it conflicts with your well-laid plans. God may wish to use you for his own good purposes. His wish may sound like an interference. It suggests a new event, a turning point in your life. At the moment of his call you feel more than ever like a creature of his.

Her next reaction was so typically human. She asked herself how? How was it possible for her to become Child-bearing if she pledged herself to remain a virgin? Assuming she received the angelic message as a bit of Good News, she still found mystery in it. Many generations of Christians have raised the question of the virgin birth. The present-day generation, so scientifically minded and so sexually permissive, may laugh at it. Some doubt it, some deny it. But none, I think, is so poignantly confronted with the question how as Mary was.

3. Acts of God

The messenger Gabriel gave her some clue but not enough to dispel the mystery of the annunciation. He promised her the shadow shape of the Holy Spirit; "the power of the Most High will cover you with its shadow." God more than once showed his people power, protection, and presence under a shadow. For Mary this was a new experience. It tested her faith in him.

God acts similarly in every life. How God acts among men is a mystery. His actions nonetheless reveal himself in shadowy forms. Faith alone discerns such actions and accepts them as they appear. As St. Paul states, "it is all part of the way the eternal God wants things to be." "He alone is wisdom."

Mary was given two assurances that God wasn't double-dealing. The first was that "nothing is impossible to God." Man can think and try the impossible, but not God. He supported the first guarantee with the news that Mary's elderly cousin Elizabeth was already pregnant six months. The implication here is that if the almighty God could make a sterile woman bear a child, he could make a Virgin bear one too.

4. Mary decides

After the disturbing and questioning interlude, Mary was ready and willing to make her decision for Christ: "Let what you have said be done to me." Once the decision was made, God gave her "the strength to live according to" it. She was favored by God *anew*, not as though she had never been favored before. God's word to and action upon Mary gave her a new understanding of herself and her role in life.

Mary didn't claim mastership over her own life. She wasn't selfish or presumptuous, trying to organize it independently of God, to obtain security for herself.

Real freedom grows out of "the obedience of faith," a free obedience. Arbitrary freedom is a delusion which makes one prone to lusts and passions. A decision that says no to God is a hollow freedom.

5. My decision

What the annunciation meant for Mary it can mean

for us, on a smaller scale. It made a difference for her in time and eternity. The same Word which came to Mary resounds to us, calling for our decision as it did for hers. Each of us should ask himself, "Am I only a spectator at the annunciation or a participant?"

My belief in God's word is for real not simply when I profess my faith in the creeds but when I actually believe God is acting in my life as I surrender myself to his power. He speaks to me and acts on me here and now. What he's doing I don't know yet, but I trust faithfully he knows that what he's doing is important for me, and I must ask him what he wants. Everything's possible for him as long as I decide in his favor.

CHRISTMAS SEASON

Solemnity of Christmas
Is 62:11-12; Ti 3:4-7; Lk 2:15-20

Your Saviour Comes

1. Born of kindness and love

We gather today to celebrate the birthday of Jesus, as we do annually. Jesus himself, however, didn't celebrate many birthdays. He came and he went, not even attaining the normal age of man.

How are we to celebrate his birthday? With faith and joy, for this is how we pray to his Father after Communion: "With faith and joy we celebrate the birthday of your Son. Increase our understanding and our love of the riches you have revealed in him."

His riches are revealed in the kindness and love of God. Yes, we celebrate the birth of the kindness and love of God in the little Jesus. Jesus just doesn't participate or share in the divine kindness and love, he *is* it. God's kindness and love appear even before our hearts are able to love him; he makes it possible for us to reciprocate with our love. His love begets ours.

How so? Because Jesus revealed himself in the form of man, not of angel. Had he taken an angelic instead of a human form he wouldn't have been able to do for us as much as he did. "For it was not the angels he took to himself; he took to himself descent from Abraham. It was essential that he should in this way become completely like his brothers. . ." (Heb 2:16f.). In order for us to receive the gift of his birth he had to be born like us, and we like him.

2. The good of creation

The birthday of Jesus recalls the story of the creation of man. In the book of Genesis we read: "God created man in the image of himself, in the image of God he created him, male and female he created them" (1:27). The act of creation marks the birthday of man. When God finishes with his work of creation, he looks it all over, especially his creation of man, and considers it very good. One would think that at this moment the kindness and love of God appear and need not appear again. But we know how man through pride and disobedience lost favor with God, and God was forced to withold much of his kindness and love for a while.

3. The new birth

Then in a new birth of kindness and love he relented. The new birth brings to us not just a new man but the Maker and Saviour of the world himself. Jesus, our Saviour and God, identifies himself with us—he is born like you and me. He makes human life livable once again through the birthday gift of his kindness and love. "Look, your saviour comes, the prize of his victory with him, his trophies before him." Since we are his prize and trophies, how wonderful his birthday is for us.

The new birth of man in Jesus reveals a greater kindness and love of God than in the first instant of creation. The kindness and love of the little Jesus are henceforward inseparable from us. His birthday "is a figure, promise, or pledge of our new birth, and it effects what it promises. As He was born, so are we born also; and since He was born, therefore we too are born. As He is the Son of God by nature, so are we sons of God by grace; and it is He who has made us such" (John Henry Newman, "The Mystery of Godliness," *Parochial and Plain Sermons,* V).

4. Baby-sit with Jesus

The crib before this altar calls to mind this truth of our faith. Tradition says we have Francis of Assisi to thank for the practice of setting up cribs at Christmas. As the story goes, he surprised the villagers of Greccio, Italy, one Christmas, when he arranged a crib for them in a mountain grotto. A live ox and a little ass were led into it. The children and their parents stood by wide-eyed to seek out the Infant Jesus in the empty crib. Francis sang the gospel story of the Nativity, then went over to the crib and with outstretched arms gazed at the empty crib. In an intense moment of desire, he saw in a vision the Baby Jesus lying there before him. The Babe reached out toward him, and Francis took him into his arms. He laid the Babe back in the crib and then began to speak to the children and their parents about the beauty and the goodness of the Babe—of God who had become the child and brother of poor human beings.

Let us keep the beautiful birthday custom of offering a gift. What birthday gift can we present to him who now has need of nothing but who once had no place to lay his head, who was born in a cave-stable, wrapped in swaddling clothes and laid in a manger? We ought to baby-sit with Jesus this Christmas as the shepherds did the first Christmas night.

5. Hurry in astonishment

As soon as the shepherds heard the good news of his birth, they "hurried away" from their flocks to him. Do we react in the same way they did, or do we equate "hurrying away" with "Do your Christmas shopping early"? The less commercialization of Christmas we allow ourselves, the more likely we will turn our thoughts upon the mystery of this great and unique event of his birth and desire its meaning.

The shepherds "repeated" what they had heard and seen, and they "astonished" others with it. What is the topic of our conversation at Christmas? And are we astonished at the right things—not so much at the glitter and glamour of man-made things, at what Santa Claus has brought, as at those things which God has wrought for our sake, at his kindness and love which will never fade? The shepherds left their flocks by night and "found Mary and Joseph, and the baby lying in the manger." Or do we prefer the material things of this world to the firstborn of all creation?

Last of all, the shepherds returned to their flocks "glorifying and praising God" for the gift of the newborn Christ. Theirs, after all, was the finest return anyone can make on the occasion of Christ's birthday—the glory and praise of God.

Feast of the Holy Family
Si 3:2-6, 12-14; Col 3:12-21; Lk 2:22-40

The Happily Married

The other day a former student of mine whose marriage I witnessed left me a note as she and her husband passed through the city on their way to visit relatives and friends. We missed seeing each other. The note read in part: "We're *very* happily married. When you do something, you do it right!" A sweet compliment, but I deserve no credit for their happy marriage. I asked myself, why do some marriages bring joy, others sorrow? Reasons? The reasons appear on this annual feast of the Holy Family.

1. Wisdom for the family

The Bible is full of tidbits of wisdom which make for happy marriages. One such tidbit is the reading from the book of Sirach or Ecclesiasticus. A rabbi colleague called my attention to the fact that the Jewish Bible doesn't contain this book, and he lamented the loss of it to us Catholics.

In Sirach the duties toward parents follow immediately upon the duties toward God. The passage serves as a commentary on Exodus 20:12. "Honour your father and your mother so that you may have a long life in the land that Yahweh your God has given to you." The two duties, toward God and parents, are fused together inseparably. One who breaks the law of love, respect, and obedience to parents is like a blasphemer. Breaking the law permits no excuse.

On the other hand, this is the only law that promises a tangible reward: rich blessings flowing from God to children. They'll have a long and (by implication) happy life in their native land. The link between parents and home country is very noticeable here. The divine blessings that come to a home and make it happy overflow into the country of our birth. Our country is the happier for its happy homes.

2. A family charter

The vein of Hebraic wisdom runs through Paul's instructions to the Colossians. "Let the message of Christ, in all its richness, find a home with you." From the rules of Christian conduct he turns to the morals for home and family. Both rules and morals originate with God. God loves you, hence you must extend that love to others. He forgives you, "now you must do the same." Christian responsibility is always reciprocal. Peace, gratitude, joy are the rich benefits that God bestows along with a long life.

This Colossian passage charters the happy home life. Where is the Christian life to develop if not in the home? The home, not the school or the church, is its center. Nothing can replace the home for the warmth, tenderness, and intense personal qualities that nourish Christian growth. Take a second look at the Pauline charter for happy home life. How much better it pictures home life than what is cartooned in the incompetent Dagwood Bumstead and Dennis the Menace. The comics, TV soap operas are eyesores compared with Bible-reading.

3. The first family

The Hebraic wisdom of Sirach and Colossians finds a living expression in the family of Jesus, Mary, and Joseph. The family ideal is lived by the first, oldest, and most important family of Christendom. How many families look to it for example, inspiration, and help? Perhaps the differences between the Holy Family and today's family are too great to overcome. Perhaps the small family size of Nazareth can't transmit its values and ethics to the industrialized and liberalized family of our culture.

Mary and Joseph showed respect for authority. "When they had done everything the Law of the Lord required," only then did they return to their hometown. They thereby instilled the same devotion to duty in Jesus. They offered in the Jerusalem temple a pair of turtledoves, one dove for the worship of God, another for the sacrifice for sin. The offering they made according to their means was an offering of the poor.

The life of the Holy Family had two centers, their home in Nazareth and the temple. The life of the Christian family today has four centers: home, workplace, school, and church. You might even add a fifth for recreation. Industrialized society brought this about. Family life today is much more mobile than it was for Joseph and his family. His home was a place where he not only ate and slept but worked, recreated, prayed, and educated the Child Jesus. Because of its mobility, family life today may lose genuine closeness. The family is called "nuclear" today in an ironic sense. Made up of a small nucleus it can, like a small bomb, split up into several parts.

4. Happy family life

Small as the first family of Christendom was, it was an "extended" family such as many groups experienced in earlier times. Grandfathers and grandmothers, uncles and aunts, all were counted in it. They all had a part to play in the development of Christian family life. Now, due to changed circumstances beyond our control, as soon as we step out of the family circle, we're likely to encounter impersonality, anonymity, and harshness. Joseph and Mary feel themselves to be total strangers in the temple. They had "Uncle" Simeon and "Aunt" Anna to give them the benefit of a wisdom accumulated through years of experience.

Every family here today can catch the spirit and wisdom of happy family life from the trio of Jesus, Mary and Joseph. They'll extend themselves to you if you pray to them for this favor. Their feast calls for a celebration in the home. Children receive no better birthday present than happily married parents. One happy marriage leads to another. "Especially in the heart of their own families, young people should be aptly and seasonably instructed in the dignity, duty, and work of married love" (*Constitution on the Church in the Modern World*, no. 49).

Solemnity of Mary, Mother of God
Nb 6:22-27; Ga 4:4-7; Lk 2:16-21

Woman of Faith

1. Our heritage

The pastoral letter of the American bishops on the Blessed Virgin Mary, titled "Behold Your Mother," has an appendix which briefly relates Mary's place in American Catholic history. It reads in part:

> The England of penal times was an unlikely point of origin for an American colony where religious toleration would prevail and Catholics would publicly profess their faith, even their devotion to St. Mary. Yet George Calvert, a convert to Catholicism and the first Lord Baltimore, was given a charter to found the crown colony of Maryland, where religious freedom would be guaranteed. When he died in 1632, his sons carried the project through. Their two ships, *The Ark* and *The Dove*, landed in Maryland (named for the queen), March 1634. Their Chaplain, Rev. Andrew White, S.J., recorded how the Catholics of the group consecrated the future colony to Our Lady of the Immaculate Conception. They called their first settlement and capital "St. Mary's City," and they named the Chesapeake "St. Mary's Bay."
>
> A Son of Maryland, John Carroll, was the first bishop of the United States. Consecrated bishop in 1790 on the feast of the Assumption, he placed his newly founded diocese of Baltimore under the patronage of Mary.

On this solemnity of the Mother of God we recall that this our mother country is dedicated to Mary, and the exact spot we stand on is the land of Mary. The truth of our heritage is borne upon us today.

2. The perfect believer

The bishops' document, subtitled "Woman of Faith,"

brings home to us who have Mary for our patroness *why*
Mary was chosen to be the Mother of the Savior and our
mother. To have faith is to trust in the will of God, and
this faith Mary had to a supreme degree. The bishops
call her "the perfect believer." Mary was full of faith
because she "could face and accept the hidden future
bound up with being Virgin Mother of the Messiah" (p.
51). In consenting to become the mother of Jesus, "let
what you have said be done to me," she stepped into a
future that was a mystery to her. At that moment she
became, together with her Son, instrumental in our becoming sons of God and heirs of salvation.

On account of this decision of hers to trust in the will
of God for her the bishops point to her as "our *mother* in
faith," singling her out among all the believers in the New
Testament as the "great Gospel model of faith."

3. Faith in Mary

The Christian faith in its fullness has more for its
object or content than a belief in Christ, Lord and Savior.
It comprises the principal teachings of Jesus and his
Church, one of which is a belief in Mary the Mother of
God. The true and full Christian must have a "faith in or
devotion to Mary." The mysteries of the rosary go to show
how the two, Jesus and Mary, are linked together in life
and destiny. As the bishops said, "Almost all of these relate saving events in the life of Jesus, episodes in which
the Mother of Jesus shared."

The bishops, of course, encourage us in the recitation
of the rosary, but they also suggest experimentation with
"new sets of mysteries," especially those which relate to
the whole public life of Jesus. One such incident is the
marriage feast of Cana, uniquely told by the evangelist
John (2:1-12). Mary has a clear grasp and command of
a situation where a young couple is about to suffer an
embarrassment. They have no more wine for their cele-

bration. Mary has a motherly concern for them, and takes pity upon them. "Do whatever he tells you," she says to the servants. Jesus at first objects, not out of disrespect to his mother, by calling her "woman," but because this isn't his hour.

4. The hour of trial

In the Johannine gospel the word "hour" has a special connotation, referring to Jesus' passion and death. It makes the marriage feast of Cana almost coincidental to that future event when Mary will stand by the side of her Son in his last agony (Jn 19:25-27). At Cana Mary placed faith or trust in the power of her Son, recognizing in him a trait of kindness and divine resourcefulness. At the foot of the Cross Mary wasn't left in the lurch by her Son. She had taken care of him up to the moment of his public life, now he saw to it that she was placed in good hands. "Woman, this is your son." John represents the entire Church, all the sons of God to whom Mary is given as a mother.

If we're to care for and give honor to Mary, we have no better way than to imitate her in hearing the word of God and doing his will. She listened attentively to the word of God spoken to her by his messenger, and she accepted it in a spirit of faith. God was asking her to be the Mother of his Son. All of us can't imitate her in her motherhood, though as sons we can ask for her spirit of faith in accepting and accomplishing God's will. John Henry Cardinal Newman recommended this, "More blessed is it to do God's will than to be God's Mother."

5. A relationship through faith

At first hearing this statement might seem to be derogatory to Mary's motherhood, and yet the truth of the matter is that without faith Mary would never have become the Mother of God. Moreover, the statement can hardly be false because it paraphrases Jesus' own words on a public occasion. His mother and companions sent word to him that they were waiting outside for him. His reply was, "Who are my mother and my brothers?" Then he added, pointing to his audience, "Anyone who does the will of God, that person is my brother and sister and mother" (Mk 3:31-35).

And once while he was speaking and a woman in the crowd paid tribute to his mother, he replied, "Still happier those who hear the word of God and keep it" (Lk 11:28).

To the degree that we live our life in a spirit of Christian faith, we turn into the sons of God, the mothers, brothers, and sisters of Christ. In a real sense our Christian faith begets faith in others around us. Because of Mary we have faith in her Son, and because of that same faith we can help others in the family of the Christian faith.

Solemnity of the Epiphany
Is 60:1-6; Ep 3:2-3, 5-6; Mt 2:1-12

Do Him Homage

1. Star-gazers

With a little touching up, the story of the magi might be made into a page of an astrology magazine or book, or like a daily horoscope. The story fits the once and still popular belief that every child is represented by a star or planet which appears at its birth. The magi seem to have been astrologers from Mesopotamia, hence skilled in occult knowledge and power.

Their story doesn't imply that the life of the Christ-Child is shaped by the position of the star at his birth. It's the other way around—the star is his, he shaped and controlled it. The ancient East saw gods in the stars. Not so the magi and their star; it beamed upon the birthplace of the God-man Jesus Christ. It shone for the magi at the right time only because his birthplace was foretold by the prophet Micah. ". . . a star from Jacob takes the leadership" (Nb 24:17); the real star is the Davidic King and Messiah. Had not the Scriptures and the Creator inspired the magi upon their course, they would have lost their way.

2. A newborn King

Nor were the magi starry-eyed observers. Their first interest was the infant king, not the star. Astrology today leads many unenlightened individuals along the starry trail of false belief and worship. Astrology is an amalgam of superstition, folklore, starry-eyed observations, and fraud. The daily horoscope is a game, not a ritual worship. Human destiny isn't hitched to a star. This is one truth the wise men from the East can teach us.

They were wise in not being led astray by a star.

Alerted and guided by it, they made their way to the
Infant Jesus. "The sight of the star filled them with de-
light," the sight of the Child Jesus filled them with adora-
tion. First the heavens bore witness to and gave homage
and service to the newborn King, then the magi followed
suit. The uncommon spectacle of the star opened their
eyes but didn't obscure their minds. By divine enlightenment they saw the significance of the mysterious star.

The same can't be said of Herod and the Israelite
priests and scribes. In contrast to the magi who, truly
believing, did the Infant homage, Herod was jealous and
saw in him a threat to his own kingship. The priests and
scribes were well versed in the Scripture but blind to its
real meaning. The magi unite true belief and worship.
The others neither believe nor worship.

3. A light to the nations

The theme of the epiphany is the appearance of Christ,
continuing and developing the theme of Christmas. It pro-
longs the joy of Christmas. Christ is declared by a satellite
star to the whole universe. He wants to be known by all
peoples and not merely by a privileged few—Mary, Joseph,
Elizabeth, John the Baptist. He reveals himself to the magi
who represent all peoples. In the epiphany we celebrate
the beginnings of our Christian vocation, our faith and the
blessed hope of an eternal inheritance.

For St. Leo the Great who left behind seven sermons
on the Epiphany, its mystery is a mystery of *light*. Christ
is the light who enlightens every man coming into this
world. We Christians see through the starlight to the
guiding light of Christ. Epiphany is for us the manifesta-
tion of the ineffable mercy of God to a fallen race, a sinful
people.

Imagine yourself atop the star of Bethlehem, from
whose height you have a world-view. That's exactly the
outlook the Isaian text presents. Phoenicia, Greece, Egypt,

Arabia are mentioned there in order to widen our view. We're to foresee nations gathering round Jerusalem to worship the God of Israel.

4. Children of light

We should count ourselves among these nations, for we're children of faith descendant from Abraham. Abraham was told, "Look up to heaven and count the stars if you can. Such will be your descendants" (Gn 15:5). We're the first spiritual heirs promised to Abraham.

The comparison of ourselves to stars must be broadened. As stars give light, so should we be starlets lighting up the way to Christ. We Gentiles have a definite contribution to make to the people of God (Is 60:5). As God's grace is shown to Paul for the sake of others (Ep 3:2), so is ours. "Be children of light" in your belief and worship, "for the effects of light are seen in complete goodness and right living and truth" (Ep 5:8, 9).

The magi came bearing gifts worthy of the Infant Jesus. They offered him incense to do him homage as God, myrrh because he was a man, and gold for his kingship.

5. Bearing gifts

The worthiest gift we present to the Christ is our spirit of faith and worship. We're asked to contribute to the financial support of the Church, besides. Christ himself, who has no need for our material gifts, prefers our heartfelt faith and worship. If we thought this fact over more carefully, we wouldn't have so many Christians missing Sunday worship. They'd regard their worship less as a duty than as a gift to Christ.

I don't have to tell you how the Mass-absentees excuse themselves. They blame us: we don't live up to our Sunday belief and worship the rest of the week. True or not, we shouldn't let up on our belief and worship. Our critics still need this kind of example, this kind of light. The magi, after paying their homage to the King of Israel, returned home by "a different way." Why a different way? Because they didn't want to repeat their old mistakes. We propose by our Christian life-style "a different way."

Baptism of the Lord
Is 42:1-4, 6-7; Ac 10:34-38; Mk 1:7-11

The Commencement

1. In fulfillment of Isaiah

The Jordan episode, as related by Mark, resembles a commencement. The situation in either case is nearly the same. Somebody has finished his schooling and is prepared for his public career. The hoopla, the cap and gown are missing from the Jordan incident, but it has a diploma (the baptism), a commencement address (the voice from the heavens), and a symbol (the dove). Going on thirty years of age, Jesus was ready to start his public ministry and ours as well.

The Markan text dovetails nicely with the Isaian promise. In Isaiah the servant-figure of Israel blurs over into a messianic figure, which the Lord fills with a prophetic spirit. So empowered, the servant establishes and instructs mankind in justice. He goes about his task gently and without fanfare, while the Lord sustains him. Mark explains in an apocalyptic way how Christ fulfills the Isaian prophecy.

2. At the Jordan

Standing at the River Jordan during the baptism-incident, would we have seen the heavens open, the dove descend, heard the voice sound forth? Of course not. The whole incident was a personal, interior experience for Jesus. It set him upon a course from which he was never to flinch or falter.

The apocalyptic details, then, have they no signifi-

cance? They do, most certainly. Although the baptism of
Jesus didn't have the same effect as it has upon us—it
didn't wash away his own sin, for he was sinless (Heb
4:15)—it did make a difference. Jesus kept up the prophetic tradition of identifying himself with the people and
their sins. He saw in his baptism a commitment to the task
of preaching to the people, of healing them from their sins.
More important than the baptism itself was the Person
baptized and his attitude.

A voice of approval sounded from the heavens: "You
are my Son, the Beloved; my favour rests on you." The
Father was well pleased with his Son for his willingness
to assume his mission. At this moment his mission very
likely became more apparent to him. He could have seen
himself in the servant-role prophesied by Isaiah: "Here is
my servant whom I uphold, my chosen one in whom my
soul delights." In reflecting upon the lot of the prophets,
he could have realized he must suffer for the sins of others.

In retrospect, we see that Jesus was baptized in antici-
pation of his death. The baptism prepared him for his
public ministry, culminating in a blood spill which washed
away the sins of the world. Thus his public life began
and ended with two baptisms—a water-baptism and a
blood bath (Mk 10:38).

The heavens opened up as the Red Sea once parted
for the Israelites to escape from Egypt. The dove appeared, representing Israel. The fact that the heavens
opened should lead us to believe that Christ's mission is
to all peoples, not only to the Israelites.

3. The Spirit descends

The Spirit's descent at the moment of baptism was of
capital importance. We just heard how Peter interpreted
this event. "God had anointed him with the Holy Spirit
and with power, and because God was with him, Jesus
went about doing good and curing all who had fallen into

the power of the devil." Jesus was a representative man, the first to enter into the new covenant with God. As the man who walked in the prophets' footsteps, he needed the communication of the Spirit. The Spirit enlightened him, gave him incentive and courage. Without the gift of the Spirit, Jesus the prophet couldn't have sustained the wear and tear of his mission.

4. Christian life

Since Jesus' experience at the Jordan River initiated him into his public life of service, it was of the nature of a commencement. The Christian who lives his baptism, taking his baptismal promises seriously, must follow in the footsteps of Christ. He too must enter into public life, he too must give public service.

Christ could have stayed behind in his hometown of Nazareth, practicing his carpenter's trade. That wouldn't have been enough for him, either. He bestirred himself, got busy, became his Father's Son and his brother's keeper. Similarly, the Christian can't sit back and let the world go to the devil. Too many social issues summon him to action, to preaching Christian principles and ideals that will lead to solutions.

5. Christian action

Whether we're included in the count of Christian noses, really doesn't matter. Our attitude is what counts, our willingness to take sides in debatable issues, and our action toward what's right and just and good for our fellowmen. Look at all the human problems in our world today: abortion, venereal disease, divorce, atheistic humanism, war, poverty, dishonesty, drug and alcohol addiction, etc. Who can have a clean Christian conscience without taking action against present-day evils?

A sensitivity to human needs and a service to the

needy will cost suffering. Listen to the remark of a nurse married to a doctor, the mother of six children: "Suffering is the making of a man, and even more so the making of a Christian. Suffering will prevent us from adopting a self-righteous, holier-than-thou attitude."

Through the power of the Spirit alone can we bear missionary suffering, that power which equips us daily for every action. Let the Spirit do what we can't do for ourselves.

SEASON OF THE YEAR

Second Sunday of the Year
1 S 3:3-10, 19; 1 Cor 6:13-15, 17-20; Jn 1:35-42

Body-cult

1. Venereal disease

The city of Corinth was a port city, bustling with trade. A sinful city, a center of immorality. Sex was advertised by some of its citizens to be as necessary for the human body as food and drink. In his letter to them, Paul cautioned the Christians there against this propaganda.

The same word of caution is in order in our cities. And not only in our cities but globally. Sexual permissiveness and liberation are spreading like an epidemic. You have to get with it. Be a swinger. Switch partners. But how long can one play around with impunity?

The effects of free love-making are also epidemic. Sexual promiscuity is germinating venereal disease almost beyond control. The largest infectious disease, second only to the common cold, is said to be "raging" and "rampant." Estimates run from 2.2 million to 2.5 million cases per year. One out of four youths may have contracted it.

Named after Venus, the goddess of love, the disease is symptomatic of a society losing its sense of decency. VD supposedly is "the disease of people who love people," but one wonders if this is loving or taking advantage of people. Here's a social phenomenon that exhibits how the flesh has won over the spirit in our society.

In our usual way of dealing with sins against the human body, we don't look for the deep human causes but for medical remedies, cures and controls. VD control funds total $43 million; the actual costs are estimated at $364 million. Naturally, the figures change yearly.

2. The body takes toll

Our bodies are the most precious, delicate and complex communicators we have. No computer can vie with the human body for complexity. Its complexity only illustrates how the body shares in the total mystery of life.

Whenever and whichever way we pervert the use of the body, it reacts in kind. Try to defy the law of bodily gravity and see what happens. If we attempt to live in a perverted paradise, the body, a communicator of disease and death, poisons everyone that comes in contact with it. It can't hide for long or unmistakably the sins committed against it. Not all the birth control pills and contraceptive devices on the market will prevent an abused body from taking its toll.

Take sexual love for an example—part of the beauty, joy, and peace within marriage. Pre-marital or extra-marital sex, on the contrary, runs the risk of racking the body in pain. Rather than communicate genuine love, the body then exposes itself to hateful feeling. The give-and-take of VD is mostly the consequence of two people communicating who have no right to do so. One diseased person alone, with a perverted sense of love, can begin a chain of infection. True love is communicative but not contagious.

3. Respect for the body

Medicine has yet to come up with a vaccine that will prevent VD. The only reliable preventive is the practice of self-discipline or self-control along with a Christian respect for the human body. Christians have had to contend in the past with Gnostics, Montanists, Albigensians, all of whom disparaged the human body as material, hence as an evil thing. Christians have always defended the nobility of the body. Flesh and spirit complement and complete each other in man and unite in a beautiful and harmonious unity. But the two can also cause each other tension and conflict, as though not belonging to one and the same person. They conflict if the spirit of man doesn't keep his bodily drives under control.

Paul's first Corinthian letter shows the highest esteem for the human body. "The body is not meant for fornication; it is for the Lord, and the Lord for the body . . . you should use your body for the glory of God." God's property, the body can't be used as we please. Because Christ bought and paid for it at the price of his own life, it is sacred.

4. The body-person

The body signifies and represents the whole human personality. No person-to-person relationship is possible without it. Bodily activity helps man to become aware of the world around him and of human associations. What would an infant do if it had no body for a medium of communication with its mother and father?

Because the human body so encloses the whole human personality, the latter is deeply affected by anything the former does. Sexual acts affect the personality deeply. They demoralize and degrade if they occur outside a proper relationship. And they spiritualize husband and wife within the sacrament of marriage.

5. The mystical body

As long as he remains earthbound, no direct spiritual

communication is possible between one man and another. Even in the Holy Eucharist we take up a bodily-personal relationship with the risen Christ. He transforms these disease-prone bodies into spiritual bodies like his own. The Eucharistic Lord esteems them so much that he nourishes them unto everlasting life.

As Paul thinks of them, our bodies are joined together into an intimate mystical relationship. They make up our membership in the body of Christ, that social body which is his Church. Christians who sin against their bodies produce a double effect. They not only desecrate the image of Christ in themselves, they also prostitute the body of the Church. Our bodies are never so noble, so grand, so beautiful as when they serve the Lord and give glory to him.

Third Sunday of the Year
Jon 3:1-5, 10; 1 Cor 7:29-31; Mk 1:14-20

Conversion

1. The Story of Jonah

The one and only appearance of the prophet Jonah in the Sunday readings makes such a delightful fish story, we should linger over it. The plot is very simple. Jonah is called by God to preach conversion to the sinful Ninevites. Seeing no reason why the God of Israel should be merciful to foreigners, he obstinately refuses and lams out on a ship run by pagan sailors. A storm blows up and threatens to capsize them. The sailors learn why—Jonah's trying to escape his duty. With an ecumenical prayer for mercy to the Israelite God for throwing Jonah overboard, the sailors calm their fears. A big fish swallows Jonah, then nauseated with the angry fellow, vomits him on the Ninevite shore where he has to convert the non-Hebrew sinners.

There are so many angles to this fish story. Take Jonah, whose story, but not his name, is fantasized. Jonah is as obstinate toward God as Israel. He personifies and represents Israelites in believing they have a monopoly upon God. In their common belief, God should exclude everybody but themselves from his mercy. Jonah resists the divine call and never has a change of heart. He complies with God's will because he has to. To speak about an individual conversion in his case is a distortion of the story. His conversion, if anything at all, is very, very reluctant, under physical and moral pressure.

2. Mass conversion

The citizens of Nineveh, on the other hand, are surprisingly changeable. Their story of conversion is reminiscent of Jeremiah 18:8, which is delivered to Israel: "But if this nation, against which I have pronounced sentence, abandons its wickedness, I then change my mind about the evil which I had intended to inflict on it." The Ninevites don't spare themselves in the process of conversion, in their "efforts to renounce their evil behaviour."

Their mass conversion is the kind of response every Church needs to undergo periodically. The name "Church" is derived from the Greek *ekklesia,* which means the community of those God calls. The Church, composed of men and women who keep on sinning, is always in need of reform. While the Ninevites struggle at conversion, the first recruits to the Church of Christ (Simon Peter and Andrew, James and John) seem to find theirs easy and instantaneous. Christ calls at once, and they follow at once. But is this so? On the contrary, the Marken gospel emphasizes how Christ is discovered by his companions. Despite an impression of spontaneous conversion, in itself it's a slow, tortuous process not everybody accepts en masse.

3. The divine call

God's role in the Jonah story is comforting to sinners, contrary to the picture of a God who is unchangeable, unrelenting, whose plans and ways are irreversible. God does change his mind! He makes moral demands upon his people, no doubt, but once they show him obedience, he relents at seeing their sincere efforts. His merciful power works upon us as clay in a potter's hand. If a vase or vessel he forms comes out wrong, he can always start afresh and do it over.

God's call for conversion isn't always as forceful as it appears in the Jonah story. He respects human freedom. And yet his call carries a power within itself, so that the response isn't all man's doing. We see how God acts in

Christ. When Jesus summons the first four, he creates his followers. Conversion is an act of God, a gift from him.

His call challenges, upsets, changes man from within, re-makes him. It happens when man finds himself in a crisis, when he comes to grips with himself, faces up to himself, his moral and spiritual situation. He has to alter his way of thinking and listen to a new message. Formerly, he may have felt distraught, torn in many ways, self-divided, broken in spirit. The change-over takes place especially when God calls man for a particular work involving the destiny of others besides himself. Imaginatively, then, Jonah discovers himself in the belly of a big fish. Realistically, Peter and Andrew, James and John become "fishers of men." The same thing may happen to parents who neglect their faith until their children come along to convert them.

4. Its urgency

God's children are called to at least one conversion. Born of Christian families, presumably one conversion should be enough for us. The seed of the Christian life should mature steadily and gradually into adolescence and maturity. More confirmed in the faith, more committed to the Christian way of life. Christian conversion is a lifelong process. The first step has to be taken like a plunge into cold water. Baptized in infancy, taught in childhood, tried in adolescence, and readjusted in manhood or womanhood.

The Pauline writing and the Markan gospel describe how urgent every conversion is. "Our time is growing short . . . the world as we know it is passing away . . . the time has come, and the kingdom of God is close at hand. Repent, and believe the Good News." The call *is* urgent, the response ordinarily takes longer. The sequence of repentance and faith in the Markan gospel isn't accidental. Faith is the essential ingredient in conversion, which takes

time to grow. We do have to detach ourselves from possessions and family ties as the first disciples did. Christian
death is the final break with the world as we know it.

The story of Jonah teaches a lesson in mercy and
conversion. What difference will it make in our Christian
lives till we hear it again?

Fourth Sunday of the Year
Dt 18:15-20; 1 Cor 7:32-35; Mk 1:21-28

Prophetic Ministry

1. Futurologist and prophet

A news columnist very cleverly coined the term "futuriasis" for the epidemic he observed sweeping the country in the 1970s. He defined futuriasis as the abnormal concern for what is about to be, fear of the future, inability to plan ahead, belief in one's ability to foretell or predict. His purpose was to spoof the genius forecasters who are cropping up in this decade. As the pace of change speeds up, futurologists want to see and plan ahead to prevent future shock.

Now the fact is that "great human minds have always looked to the future, sensed coming events, warned their contemporaries of the future, consequences of the deeds of the present" (Karl Rahner, *Visions and Prophecies*, p. 97). But their predictions, true or false, were worth no more than the evidence they could produce, that is, they rested on how they analyzed the present. Their forecasts were sometimes no more trustworthy than the weatherman's.

2. How they differ

Is it possible that we're experiencing a revival of prophetism? Hardly. The role of the prophet is quite dissimilar to that of the contemporary futurologist. The prophet mediates between God and man, he speaks out for God his words with his authority. The futurologist, with no concern for God, thinks the future won't take care of itself, so he forecasts and plans. How then are we to interpret the promise foretold by Moses: "Yahweh your God will raise up for you a prophet like myself. . .?" Prophecy was God's gift to Moses and to the whole line of prophets culminating in Christ.

Futurologists and news analysts attempt to predict the future in great and precise detail. CBS radio proposes to tell us all about the 21st century. The prophet doesn't dare to. His message is future-oriented all right, but he intends to show God to be the Lord of history, that the future lies in his hands. When the Lord of history gives information about the future, his word lends meaning to it but leaves the details obscure. Man therefore remains free to work out his own future *under God.* God triumphs where man proves weak and helpless.

Unlike the futurologist who hopes to make the future rosy, the prophet issues a warning if necessary. He discerns whether a human policy or practice fits into salvation history, namely, whether it's truly salvific for man. The Marxist prophet paints a future utopia for the workingman; the Christian prophet warns against conceiving of a kingdom of heaven upon earth. The true prophet calls the shots as he sees them, with divine help. He promises no pot of gold at the end of the rainbow since there is none. He won't do away with the daily cross which stands even in the secret, dark future.

3. Jesus the prophet

A typical day in the ministry of Jesus illustrates how prophecy differs from futurolgy. Jesus teaches in the synagogue and impresses his audience. They sense that "here is a teaching that is new . . . and with authority behind it." His teaching, supported with divine authority, is ripened and received enthusiastically. The scribes can't best him in teaching because they speak only with human authority.

Jesus is the New Moses, the teacher of the New Law

who sums up and supersedes Old Testament prophecy. His authority is to teach *and* to heal. He has power to overthrow satan's rule. His word exorcises the demonic element in the world and in human life. One word of his—"Be quiet! Come out of him!"—reduces the power of evil to nothing. Jesus confirms his prophecy with a miracle, which is more than can be said of other prophets.

4. Prophecy in the Church

Prophecy, however, endures in the Church Jesus founded. The Church is a prophetic community; her nature is to speak out for God. This permanent gift she exercises for the good of the human community. The Church will always have prophets who read into events, see whatever is true or false in them, and warn us to make wise judgments and decisions in the present so as to shape the future of God's kingdom. Pope John XXIII, Sir Thomas More, and Joan of Arc were prophets in their day.

The lot of the prophet in the Church isn't easy. Before we can prophecy, we must make sure we listen carefully to God's word. "The man who does not listen to my words that he speaks in my name, shall be held answerable to me for it." God won't deal lightly with the prophet who *presumes* to speak in his name. This is why Paul advises the would-be prophets in the Corinthian community to give their undivided attention to the Lord. Total concentration on his word and dedication to his service, which prophecy requires, can't be distracted with other interests. Listening with a divided heart and attention, we can't be certain that God is speaking.

5. Social criticism

After listening to God especially in prayer, the prophet among us still has to speak out. Sometimes Jesus and his Church must speak out against societal evils. The two per-

form the function of social critics. The prophetic voice
then carries the overtones of protest. Don't think that
registering a protest goes down well with the people we in
good conscience protest against. The demonic element in
society has a voice of its own, which will try to drown
us out.

We won't heal the ills of society unless we speak out
courageously, trusting that God will apply his healing
power where he sees fit. We'll have to pray and repent as
we speak out, for such is the way of all prophecy. In some
instances (poverty, birth control, abortion, dishonesty),
where the futurologists do nothing but predict, we have
to protest.

Fifth Sunday of the Year
Jb 7:1-4, 6-7; 1 Cor 9:16-19, 22-23; Mk 1:29-39

Fruits of Labor

1. Labor problems

What happens to Job, Paul, Peter's mother-in-law, and Jesus—to all who figure in the biblical readings today—probably happens to many of us. They all experience a labor crisis, all are hurting because of their situation, As we shall see, the labor itself isn't causing them suffering, or making them feel ill at ease, as much as the fruits of their labor. The labor leaves them with a bitter taste. Why?

Life and work in the big city is a bureaucratic ant-heap. Workingmen are scurrying about, too busy to enjoy the fruits of their labor. A growing dissatisfaction is infiltrating the ranks of blue-collar and white-collar workers. A sense of social consciousness is developing particularly along the mass-production factory line that finds work degrading, dehumanizing. Workers feel they're nothing but tools in a machine age. Losing their idealism, they adopt an I-don't-care attitude. Their life is becoming a job-centered thing. Why shouldn't their work be more attractive and meaning-ful, giving them a greater satisfaction and sense of achieve-ment? Why not?

The production, distribution, consumption of the fruits of the earth are resulting in huge economic problems, split-ting into rival parties the rich and the poor. Laborers are no longer content to be mere wage-earners. Why doesn't money seem to motivate them?

2. A theological gap

The basic reason for the fruits of work turning sour is

the lack in practice if not in theory of a theology of work. The time is ripe for giving more than economic considerations to work. Work is a most natural means of expressing man's unique personality. It helps man to complete himself in the image and likeness of God. Man is endowed by his Maker with the power of co-creation. He has yet to carry out the correct idea of the relationship between himself and nature.

The world of nature is entrusted to man, left for him to complete even while using it for his needs. Man is to discover in his work with nature the means of self-realization. He becomes more aware of himself through his work. It links man and nature together. He epitomizes in himself the values of the world of nature. Man is at one with his work, with the natural materials he works upon. Affecting the human standard of living and the whole way of life, work no less, if done properly, gives access to the kingdom of God. Man employs this-worldly materials and conditions to help build the new heavens and the new earth.

Failure to observe a theology of work eventually leads man to his own undoing. Present-day problems with labor, pollution, exploitation of natural resources, and the conflict between workfare and welfare result from this failure.

3. Job

Job in his soliloquy bemoans the fact that his life and labor are full of misery. He wonders why. Though his story dates back probably to the fifth century B.C., he sounds like a twentieth-century worker who has lost his good fortune. Sitting on a dung-heap, symbol of the collapse of his little world, and in a black mood, Job cries out. Like a workman engaged in "hired drudgery," "sighing for the shade"—rest and recreation. He has "no thought but his wages." For some men and women in this workaday world, Job's "months of delusions" have turned into years, and swifter than an assembly line their "days have passed, and vanished, leaving no hope behind."

Job is tortured by satan and tested by the Lord. Many a jobholder today feels the same treatment at the hands of capitalistic and communistic lords.

4. Paul

Paul the preacher of the Good News has his work cut out for him. It affords him no rights, only duty and responsibility. He has no complaint about this. In fact, he enslaves himself not for economics but to win converts to Christ. Such is his overriding motive, and nothing else matters much, not even the inconvenience and losses to himself.

Yet human as he is, Paul is sad over the meager visible effects of his work, sacrifice, and preaching. His labor is to change the hearts of men. Not too many are converting. He feels fortified in his efforts nonetheless by the prospects of gospel blessings for both his people and himself. His concern is for the people's good.

5. Peter's mother-in-law

Peter's mother-in-law gets up completely recovered, saved by Christ, and serves a meal to the guests—a very humane deed. The incident of her cure and its consequences are so simply and quickly told in the Markan gospel that we may miss its twofold lesson.

Her healing is to be taken as a sign of Jesus' redemptive work. He heals sickness more easily than sin. His redemptive purpose is to heal us from sin so that all we do will have a redeeming effect. He treats us right so that we in turn treat everything and everybody else right. Redemption means humanization. The meal Jesus serves us in the Eucharist is a very human gesture.

The cure of Peter's mother-in-law is one of many Jesus performs in the city of Capernaum. His reputation as a

wonder-worker travels fast. Not one to seek popularity,
Jesus doesn't want his works misunderstood. His miracles
are stirring wrong messianic hopes in some hearts, and this
he won't have. So he runs off.

But not before arising and praying by himself long
before dawn. We should see in this little detail of his life
and work a cure for our labor problems. We aren't going
to solve them unless we take time off our work to pray, to
ask God for help, to offer our labor to him, to reflect upon
the redemptive motive of all we do.

Sixth Sunday of the Year
Lv 13:1-2, 44-46; 1 Cor 10:31-11:1; Mk 1:40-45

Feeling Sorry

1. Faith-healing

How much stock should one put in faith-healing? Faith-healing in itself is defensible, but how genuine are all the reported faith-healings? The Kathryn Kuhlmann Foundation, a non-profit charitable organization with headquarters in Pittsburgh, Pa., has any number of miracle stories to relate over a period of twenty-five years. Its foundress, Kathryn Kuhlmann, very modestly disclaims any credit for faith-healing. "I am not a modern-day seer nor am I worker of miracles. . . No one knows better than I that in myself I am nothing. I am not your point of contact. I am not a deliverer. I stand before you helpless. And yet the miracles happen. Why—why?"

In her book, *God Can Do It Again,* a sequel to *I Believe in Miracles,* she ascribes numerous cures to the power, mercy, and love of God. She's so right; no earthly, human power can work divine wonders. And yet she names her meetings "miracle services" and draws the sick in large numbers. The cures she enumerates, tallied up with other faith-healings, are sufficient to boggle the mind.

Miracles are reported too at the world-famous shrines of Lourdes, Fatima, Guadalupe, and others. The Church hasn't passed any official judgment upon the miracles, though she has approved of the shrines or places of pilgrimage. They have become meeting places for the devout who manifest a spirit of faith and prayer.

2. Illness and poverty

The phenomena of faith-healing and miracle contrast
with a poor health problem, an over-medicated society,
and medical miracles over the last two decades. Medical
science has still to eradicate, if possible, heart and lung
disease, venereal disease, cancer, mental illness and retard-
ation, arthritis, blindness and deafness, cerebral palsy,
epilepsy, multiple sclerosis, muscular dystrophy, parkin-
sonism. Illness and poverty are intertwined. As one analyst
puts it, "Poverty begets disease and illness begets poverty."

3. Leprosy

Prior to and in the time of Christ, leprosy was the
generic name for all kinds of skin disease. Many cases of it
were curable; it wasn't always the severe Hansen's disease
we hear about nowadays, of which Father Damien died
during his service of the afflicted on the island of Molokai.
Jesus felt sorry for the leper, whatever his disease was, and
cured him. This little detail of "feeling sorry for him" was
added to the story of the cure by the evangelist Mark
alone. Human pity and divine power were often linked
together in the life of Jesus.

By the Mosaic Law, the leper had to give everybody
fair warning of his disease, which meant he was a religious
and social outcast. He was quarantined from society until
cured, purified, and reinstated by the priest. Primitive
society put a religious meaning upon sickness. So leprosy
was the plague of the sinner, a sign of sin. By healing the
leper, Jesus demonstrated a power superior to the Mosaic
Law and broke down the wall of division between the
clean and unclean. By sending him off to the priest, he
showed his regard for points of the Law. And by ordering
him to keep still about the cure, he prevented his messianic
identity from being leaked out yet.

We're readily horrified at the hygienic practices and
attitudes of a primitive society. Our standards won't allow
people with infectious diseases to run around in open

society. But in at least one respect our attitude toward "unpleasant people" is no better. (I've borrowed the phrase from a columnist.) What's our attitude and practice toward the "unpleasant people"—the poor, convicted, mentally ill, old, and delinquent youth? We tend to keep them out of circulation, out of sight, outside the mainstream of society. We're not feeling very sorry for them.

4. Works of mercy

Kathryn Kuhlmann and other religious leaders, whatever their motive, do welcome the sick. Kathryn Kuhlmann keeps insisting that the moral conversions of sinners are much more marvelous than physical cures. She's right again. The sinner who turns aside from his evil path and cries out to Christ for a cure, brings joy to heaven. Even more, since his cure is a change of heart, within himself, it can't always be as glamorized and sensationalized as a physical cure. God's power, mercy, and love work in the depths of a man more freely and not so openly.

Oftentimes we can't do much more in the line of treatment and cure of physical illness. The Christian, however, has a baptismal power and duty to feel sorry for fellow sinners and do everything possible to assist them. The most effective assistance we render them and anyone is taught by the apostle Paul. "Try to be helpful to everyone at all times." "Do it for the glory of God," not for some selfish motive. Paul sees himself as a model incorporating the life of Christ, giving glory to God and good example to men, facilitating their salvation and the growth of the Church. Nothing is so effective as personal good example that changes a life for the better.

Feeling truly sorry for others in their corporal and spiritual needs obliges us to works of mercy, the forms personal good example takes in any culture. Traditionally we know of seven corporal and seven spiritual works of mercy. Such forms are still very much up-to-date. Feeding the hungry, giving drink to the thirsty, clothing the poor, rehabilitating the convicted, sheltering the displaced, visiting and tending the sick, burying the dead. Correcting, teaching, counseling, comforting, bearing wrongs patiently, forgiving, and praying for the living and the dead. Feeling sorry is the next thing to taking action. We leave the working of miracles to Jesus.

Seventh Sunday of the Year
Is 43:18-19, 21-22, 24-25; 2 Cor 1:18-22; Mk 2:1-12

The Great Healer

1. Divine forgiveness

The belief of the early Church in the healing power of Christ is very evident in the Markan gospel. The first Christians awoke to the meaning of this power only after the event of the resurrection. From this vantage point they were able to see more fully through the eyes of faith and to express more clearly that Christ was gifted with divine power. His power of forgiving sins had a triple effect. It healed men of their sins; it vindicated the people's belief in the Son of God; but it also left Christ open to the charge of blasphemy. This Man was a pretender, usurping a power that belonged to God alone.

The forgiveness of sins isn't something to be taken for granted. Nobody can force it upon God. Yet God can hardly be indifferent to the sins of mankind. Already in the days of the prophet Isaiah, God felt slighted by a sinful people. "You have burdened me with your sins, troubled me with your iniquities." Mankind would have been left with the blotch of sin hadn't God in his mercy chosen to wipe it out. "I it is, I it is, who must blot out everything and not remember your sins."

The most remarkable fact about divine forgiveness is that it not only forgives but forgets. If we can't forget our sins, God can. The effects of sins, the memory of them, wrankle in our minds, driving them to distraction. So different from the human, the divine forgiveness invites us to a stronger and more self-forgetful love for God and neighbor.

The mercy the sinless Christ bestows on the paralytic was of the same variety as the divine. "My child, your sins are forgiven." The bystanders were startled more by the forgiveness of sins than by the cure of the paralytic. "Who can forgive sins but God?" To verify a moral conversion Jesus worked a physical cure. The one cure had the value of a sign for the other. Jesus wouldn't have been taken at his word had the paralytic not walked away cured.

2. What is sin?

Jesus was sinless and therefore more capable than any one of us of assessing the evil of sin. He could see it in its stark reality. The reason for his sinlessness was that he was the Yes to all God's promises and demands.

Sin is a No to God's promises and demands, to the desires and needs of our fellowmen, and to our environment. Sin is a turning away from God and a turning to something or someone else in his place. Sin is the substitution of an idol for God. Sin is a paralyzing of our heart and its efforts to orient our whole life to God.

Our life is stiff with paralysis, not the rigidity of death. Our ordinary experience of sinfulness doesn't consist of a complete and final No to God but of a Yes-and-No attitude. We let grass and weeds grow up together in our lives. How mixed up we are, how weak and evil, how we make promises and break them, how we resort to excuses, how ungenerous we are to God and our neighbor.

3. A Church forgives

Jesus is God's availability for sinners, present as a healer in the Church. In his name, the Church though sinful in some sense releases sinners from their sins. It could be asked of the Church more so than of Christ, "Physician, heal yourself" (Lk 4:23). Peter the leader in the Church who denied Christ, preached forgiveness: "It is to him that all the prophets bear this witness: that all who believe in Jesus will have their sins forgiven through his name" (Ac 10:43). Paul, too, a persecutor of the Church, pointed to Christ the healer: "It is through him that forgiveness of your sins is proclaimed" (Ac 13:38). Paradoxically, a Church of sinful men has as its head the sinless Christ to make us over, to turn us out *new*.

Christ is actively healing in the sacrament of penance. There, as in the house at Capernaum, he meets the sinner with the loving judgment of God. The meaning of the confession of sins is a meeting with Christ within the Church. Once upon a cross, Christ triumphed over sin; again and again in the Church he triumphs over it.

4. The confession of sins

The confession of sins *signifies* the fact of our sinfulness before God, makes the fact more obvious to us. One reason for the declining number of penitents is that the sign-value of confession has been lost sight of. The clearer recognition of its sign-value, the greater awareness of sinfulness. Oftentimes we can't fully express our total sinfulness which goes beyond words. Even the sins we know in particular don't entirely express what God forgives.

Only a deeper faith makes us open to the sign-value of confession. Just as faith is a prerequisite for recognizing a miracle, such as the healing of the paralytic, so is it a prerequisite of another type of healing—forgiveness. Faith in the resurrection awakened in the first Christians a keener sense of divine forgiveness. Jesus' resurrection to a new life backed up their earlier impressions of his healing power.

Our need of confessing sins is just as great as the paralytic's need of the divine healing. Sin is a punishment in itself. Which is worse—bearing the punishment of sin or confessing it? The growing tendency for many Christians is to make their confessions as *troublesome* and *rare* as letting a paralytic down through a mud roof. That mud roof is a primitive but poetic resemblance of the distance that lies between Christ the healer and sinners.

Repeated, frequent confession has the sign-value of drawing us closer to Christ just as the routine growing and living and loving together draw husband and wife closer. It mends the wounds of separation between us and God, among ourselves. Paralysis is curable once and for all; sin takes longer and oftener.

Eighth Sunday of the Year
Ho 2:16-17, 21-22; 2 Cor 3:1-6; Mk 2:18-22

New and Old

1. A letter of recommendation

Over the years, I've been asked to write numerous letters of recommendation, letters for students, the handicapped, job-seekers. Some schools and personnel offices want you to fill out their own letters. A letter of recommendation should be an honest report and appraisal, and ordinarily one doesn't have to hesitate about it.

Only once did a letter of mine backfire. I wrote a short note *not* recommending a seminarian, which his pastor took offense at and pleaded with me to change—"in a spirit of charity." I was tempted to reply No—"in a spirit of justice," but I did change the note enough to let the seminarian matriculate. Later he quit.

Were it possible or necessary to write a letter of recommendation for Christians, it would have to contain the following:

2. The true Christian

To whom it may concern, this isn't "a new attempt to commend ourselves" to anyone. Far be it from us to give a false impression, to put down on paper a description of ourselves that may not be true to reality. Total strangers may demand from us letters of recommendation, but we prefer to let them see us and judge for themselves. In reality, nothing commends us more than our qualifications.

A letter, a piece of paper, written in ink, is only as reliable and authentic as the man who signs his name on it. Personal interview or relationship most recommends the Christian. The true Christian qualifies as one who has the new law of love written on his heart, who keeps the spirit of the law rather than the letter. A man of inner grace whose heart is filled up with wisdom and love (the Hebrew *hesed*) is his own recommendation.

3. Two letters of recommendation

Thus far in the history of his correspondence with mankind, God has written three letters of recommendation. His first was on stone tablets with his handwriting spelling out man's duty to his Maker and to his fellowmen. A splendid piece of work (Ex 24:12), it taught everything man needs to know and to do in order to give a Judaeo-Christian testimony. You might ask, if it was a sure-fire means to salvation, what went wrong with it? Briefly, men either didn't abide by it or put their own strict/liberal construction on it.

Seeing that men couldn't be recommended by the former Law, God wrote a second letter of recommendation. This time not on stone tablets, as of old, but in a *new* way, on human hearts. "Deep within them I will plant my Law, writing it on their hearts. Then I will be their God and they will be my people" (Jr 31:31). At first the recommendation was put in the form of a promise, then his Spirit carried it out. Since then his Spirit inculcates the rules of Christian conduct from within. The old-time legal religion imposes rules from without.

In a sense, whatever is new or old makes no difference to God. The new strikes us as different from the old in a time sequence. But this isn't the only way to understand the difference between the two. The new in God's estimation is qualitatively better than the old. And this is how God regards his covenantal relationship to mankind. How much better it is for being written on human hearts.

4. A third letter

One human heart was so open to God's Spirit that its possessor was empowered to create all things *anew* (Heb 1:10-12). He had an authority far superior to the Mosaic Law. He personalized a new covenant with God along with a new manhood and a new commandment. He set up a new economy of love. Need I tell you that he was Christ? For this reason he was affectionately called the "bridegroom."

The bridegroom is still with us, a perfect letter of recommendation from God the Father. Truly, we Christians await the return of the bridegroom only under another form. In one form, the Eucharistic presence, Christ is always present in our midst. The recommendation of the Eucharistic Christ is found in one of the Pauline letters: "In the same way he took the cup after supper, and said, 'This cup is the new covenant in my blood. Whenever you drink it, do this as a memorial of me'" (1 Cor 11:25).

Now we see more clearly why the Church reduced the length of the Eucharistic fast. "As long as they (the bridegroom's attendants) have the bridegroom with them, they could not think of fasting." The Church cut down on the fasting and upgraded the celebration, but hasn't taken away all its value; it still has a spiritual usefulness. Ours isn't a purely spiritual religion; it needs bodily participation. Fasting, not weight-watching, is a religious act. It proves that the spirit of a man is in command and can bring the flesh humbly and dependently in God's presence.

5. The new Christian

We should think of our own role today according to the Pauline idea of exemplary Corinthians. We should be the *new* Christians with no letter of recommendation besides our Christian lives and works. This letter God is writing on our hearts, tracing out our qualifications. His qualifications outfit us not with a letter but with a Spirit.

Make no mistake about it—the best letter of recommendation to our times is the *new* Christian. The Bible serves a purpose of instruction and edification in human life, yet nothing is so renewing for society as a "biblical people." They're like new pieces of cloth you don't sew to an old cloak. Or like new wine you don't pour into old wineskins. Unless we become *new* Christians, we're going to be tossed aside like old cloaks and old wineskins. Sincerely yours in Christ.

LENTEN SEASON

First Sunday of Lent
Gn 9:8-15; 1 P 3:18-22; Mk 1:12-15

Sign of the Rainbow

1. Lent and baptism

"The Lenten Season has a twofold character: 1) it recalls baptism or prepares for it; 2) it stresses a penitential spirit. . . . In the liturgy itself and in liturgy-centered instructions, these baptismal and penitential themes should be more pronounced" (*Constitution on the Sacred Liturgy,* #109).

The liturgy of the first Sunday of Lent fits this description almost perfectly. However, baptized in infancy, how many of us have the remotest recollection of the first liturgical event in our life? We may know them from hearsay: the time and place of our baptism, the name of the priest who baptized us, the names of our sponsors. We can obtain a certificate testifying to the event noted down in the baptismal register. The sacrament of baptism itself left an enduring mark on us, and oriented our entire life to Christ the Savior.

2. Noah and ark

The saving power of baptism extends into the human past further than even our parents or sponsors can recall. According to 1 P 3:21, Noah's flood is a type prefiguring the baptism that saves us now. In short, the flood, Noah and his family of seven, and his ark make up a dramatic story of divine justice and mercy. The flood was a turning-point in the history of mankind. When men rejected God's rule, they were overwhelmed with their own sinfulness. The forty-day and forty-night flood symbolized the punishment they fell heir to. Only Noah and his family were spared. Their passage on the ark was their salvation, just as baptism is our passage through water and our salvation.

The forty-day period stands for an indefinite number and indicates that God allows time for repentance. Entering into the first explicit covenant with man, God promises Noah he'll never again destroy man. The divine promise seems so much sweeter at a time when man threatens to destroy himself with nuclear armament and pollution of land, sea, and sky. As a reminder of his promise, God suggests we look for the colorful and lovely rainbow after a rain, "a sign of the Covenant between me and the earth."

A further reminder, but of later date, is the name attached to a part of the Church building. This part where the congregation gathers is called the "nave," a term derived from the Latin *navis,* ship. In ancient art the Church was often pictured as a ship riding the waters. It was named "Noah's Ark" because, like its predecessor, it survived the water which prefigured the cleansing of man.

3. The baptismal rite

More importantly, the Church administers its sacrament of baptism occasionally during Sunday Mass, with an entire congregation witnessing and participating in it. One symbolism then comes through more plainly: baptism is an initiation into the people of God, into the community of Christ. The parents, sponsors, and congregation welcome the baptized into the Church. A new spiritual bond arises between parents and their children, and between their children and the congregation.

4. Into death and resurrection

The sacrament of baptism has significance in view of all this history and liturgy, yet it would still lack redemptive power but for one other event. Somehow through this sacrament, mysteriously, Christ incorporates us into his death and resurrection. His pierced side flooded over with water and blood that cleansed mankind of sin. At the same time his pierced arms reached out to everybody. His tomb opened up to a new life, a risen life. "When we were baptized in Christ Jesus we were baptized in his death," wrote St. Paul; in other words, when we were baptized we went into the tomb with him and joined him in death (Rm 6:3-4). Every baptism, especially baptism by immersion, symbolizes Christ's death and resurrection.

How wonderful it would be if one baptismal cleansing were sufficient for a lifetime! Then the flood waters and the resurrection would show their full power. A fantastic idea, but not new. The early Church reported how some converts to Christianity wanted to postpone their baptism till their deathbed. They planned to unite their birth into heavenly life with the death of their earthly life.

5. Lifelong repentance

Since we don't ordinarily retain our baptismal innocence, we live in need of continual repentance. Baptism, besides cleansing us from all sin, ushers us into a penitential life. Once baptized, we dare never to step out of the penitential habit. The struggle against sin would be much worse without baptism. Sad memories of a sinful past, guilt feelings we can't shake off, they prompt us to repentance. We're not quick-change artists on the scene of life. We must learn to die to our worst selves—slowly, painfully, daily. The cleansing process must go on.

After his baptism by John, Jesus went into the wilderness for forty days. The number forty in no way determined the length of his stay. The wilderness was proverbially the hangout for satan and his evil spirits. Christ met and triumphed over them on their own grounds.

He then went forth among his people to preach a gospel of repentance. The repentance he meant for us is more of a spirit than an act or Lenten series of acts. Repentance is a spirit creating change from within the heart of man. But to change from within we must work from without, in many self-disciplining ways. Rather than I suggest them to you, think of where your weaknesses lie, for there you must apply the penitential remedy.

Second Sunday of Lent
Gn 22:1-2, 9, 10-13, 15-18; Rm 8:31-34; Mk 9:2-10

Put to a Test

1. On trial

The whole of a lifetime is a test for eternity. Life on earth is a trial run for life in heaven. People are put to the one test to prove their worthiness for the other. Actually, none of us likes to be tested. School children make funny faces at the mention of tests. Within the same day, two students reacted differently to them. The one asked if the finals were optional; the other was going to write a persuasive essay against final exams. Is there really something wrong with testing, or are we just naturally fearful of the results? We try on clothes before wearing them publicly, we carry out flight tests before using planes, we sample foods before selling or buying them.

2. Covenant with Abraham

For God to put his people to a test before accepting them into his everlasting kingdom is only natural. Abraham, a patriarch or father-ruler, was tested for his faith and obedience. A main characteristic of patriarchal religion was to enter into a personal relationship or covenant with God. Abraham was a Mesopotamian, fairly old already when he became a migrant and ventured into the unknown and uncertain. God asked him to make a fresh start in a new land.

Many family traditions still retain the stories of how grandparents or earlier ancestors immigrated to this land. Such a family tradition helps us to appreciate Abraham's story. Abraham the wanderer had to bank upon God's promise even when its fulfillment seemed impossible.

The fourth Eucharistic prayer states, "Again and again you (God) offered a covenant to man. . . ." Last Sunday we noted God's covenant with Noah, this Sunday we recall the renewal of the covenant with Abraham. God covenanted with Noah as representative of the human race; he covenanted with Abraham as representative of the Hebrew people, Israel. By covenant we are to understand an agreement between two parties, a pact they have to stand by. God promised that Abraham would father a large multitude of settlers in an unfamiliar territory.

3. Trust in a promise

The first reading relates a suspenseful moment. The moment was at hand for God to keep his promise, while appearing as if he was about to break it. Abraham in his old age did become a father. His son Isaac was the only link with the far-off goal of inheriting the land of Canaan. If God truly meant Abraham to sacrifice his only son, his only hope was about to die. God stayed the knife-clutching hand in mid-air. He kept his promise.

Abraham could have protested to God about using human or child sacrifice, but he didn't. His faith in the divine promise was a firm dedication to God even when everything was against him. It took the form of obedience to the divine command that only apparently conflicted with a divine promise. The heart of the covenant faith was that God would make a great nation from Abraham's posterity. The covenant relationship was the basis of the Israelite community. Abraham was convinced that God acts to bring blessings to those who are obedient to him and punishment to those who flout his will.

Glancing back over the history of the covenant relationship with God, we see that it runs through stages. The covenant with Adam anticipates the one with Noah, Noah with Abraham, Abraham with Moses, and so on. At every stage somebody's faith is put to the test. Somebody has to trust in a future that lies only in God's hands. Then, in reward for a trustful obedience, God executes a good outcome.

4. The new covenant sacrifice

This is the story of the covenant by stages, and God doesn't throw away its plot, not even for his Son. With his Son, he enters into "a new and everlasting covenant," which is just as suspenseful and full of surprises as ever. God expects obedience from his Son. He tests him. In fulfillment of his will Jesus gives himself up to death. Jesus' dedication to the Father's will concludes with self-sacrifice. Thus the new covenant is written in Jesus' blood. No covenant, no test—it's that simple.

The history of the covenant and its testing isn't over, by any means. That history is embodied in the Mass, and in the life of every Mass participant. The Mass is "the acceptable sacrifice which brings salvation to the whole world," "a living sacrifice of praise." The Mass blends together two traditions in the making of the covenant. In the one tradition God is present at a sacred meal; in the other the covenant is made effective by a sacrifice. The ancients believed that sacrificial blood has the power of bringing two parties into a covenant. The sacrificial meal of the Mass brings us together with God through his Son.

Lent is a time for sacrifice. The Mass contains the motif of sacrifice. As Paul says, "Since God did not spare his own Son, but gave him up to benefit us all, we may be certain, after such a gift, that he will not refuse anything he can give." In the Mass we receive the transfigured Son of God and hear the Father's voice, "This is my Son, the Beloved, listen to him." "There at God's right hand he stands and pleads for us." Granted that sacrifice is a spiritual ordeal, a test we all dread, "with God on our side who can be against us?"

Third Sunday of Lent
Ex 20:1-17; 1 Cor 1:22-25; Jn 2:13-25

Law and Order

1. The commandments under fire

Twice lately I read criticisms of the Ten Command-ments—the set of laws, not the Hollywood movie by the same name. The critics, supposedly intelligent men, thought they were unsuitable laws for our society. One critic, a theologian, criticized them for being too abstract, not concrete enough to cover every situation, or not ab-stract enough to be usable as general principles of human conduct. Another critic said they were too simple. They didn't pertain to the refined ways in which we sin or commit crime nowadays. Now, is there really something wrong with the Ten Commandments?

2. The need for rules

The mass of people need rules to live by, general and simple so as to be understandable. In that respect, the Ten Commandments have no equal. The Magna Charta is a great charter of human liberties but doesn't have the all-encompassing force and value of the Decalogue. The Dec-laration of Independence and the Constitution of the United States spell out the rights and duties of a particular people, not of mankind. The Charter of the United Nations is a great document which many nations subscribe to, yet it also is limited in its sanction. What else can we turn to for universal application than the Ten Commandments?

You know what happens when man abandons or neglects the simple, straight-forward, no-nonsense laws of

God? He devises his own, of course. But then laws begin to proliferate, charters accumulate, filled with "ifs" and "buts." Along with the wordier, lengthier legislation comes disrespect for law. As soon as human conduct drifts away from the Commandments, with their simplicity and directness, man resorts to the complexity of his own laws, the multiplicity of case studies (casuistry or situation ethic), or the use of police force.

3. Covenant and commandment

A return to the study, spirit, and observance of the Ten Commandments would benefit society today. The Ten Commandments were originally known as the Ten Words God spoke to the Hebrew people. That title indicates how brief they once were. They were the heart of the Mosaic Law, then transplanted into the New Law. They set forth the meaning and purpose of all subsequent laws, which was to express the divine will for mankind. They sealed God's covenant with man.

Before God makes his will known to his people, he provides them with the motivation for abiding by it. He recalls his gracious deeds to them, how he rescued them from Egypt and led them into the promised land. They must pledge him obedience from a motive of gratitude and trust. One good turn deserves another.

The Ten Commandments are divided into two parts, religious and moral. The first three take up man's relations with God, the last seven man's relations with his fellow man. Both parts instruct us about the divine will, both deter man from evil doing. They are no *imposition*. They contain elements of the natural law, namely, of a way of life by which man can live most humanly. They sum up the basic demands of the human conscience more accurately and surely than ethical philosophers are capable of formulating. Human codes of law and the divine code differ in one essential—in the latter crime against man is likewise crime against God. God knows best what is beneficial for human existence. His laws, therefore, are grounded not in his arbitrary will but in the very nature of man. How truly then does a lawbreaker not merely take the law into his own hands but offend God and man.

4. Letter and spirit

A common complaint against the Church is that she's too institutionalized, too legalistic. She does adhere to the Ten Commandments, fundamentally. In doing so, she follows the lead of her founder Jesus Christ. She also knows that legislation can't of itself change men from within. Jesus rejected the letter of the law but enfleshed its spirit. No man offers a better example of love and obedience to the will of the heavenly Father. He cleaned the moneychangers out of the temple in a spirit of dedication to the Father.

His keeping of the Ten Commandments explains in part why "the power and wisdom of God" rested in him. The Commandments reveal divine wisdom and instill divine power in one who keeps them. They aren't any more of a pushover for Jesus than for anyone else. He knew human frailty by his own experience. That's why "he never needed evidence about any man; he could tell what a man had in him."

5. Source of happiness

Listen carefully to the conversations of people around you and you'll hear of their deep longing for law and order in our society. Naturally, there are some who crave freedom, but many more feel the need for law and order. Law and order is one benefit that accrues from the keeping of the Ten Commandments. Law makes for human freedom; lawlessness brings nothing but disorder; complex laws leave too many loopholes.

Although the Ten Commandments were probably all couched in negative language, and some still have "don'ts" in them, they all promise the positive effect of happiness. "He who listens closely to the word shall find happiness; he who puts his trust in Yahweh is blessed" (Pr 16:20).

Fortunately for our society, many people still hold to law as a source of happiness. May they prosper. God offers them this bit of encouragement: "I show kindness to thousands of those who love me and keep my commandments."

Fourth Sunday of Lent
2 Ch 36:14-17, 19-23; Ep 2:4-10; Jn 3:14-21

The Cross

1. Crucifixes, ancient and modern

Most crucifixes we see misrepresent the meaning of the cross. They show a tortured Christ hanging limp and dead on the cross. Most crucifixes symbolize an act of violence. The Christianity they signify is a gloomy, morbid ideal, with emphasis upon suffering. The cross appears mostly under the aspect of pain. We object to much violence on movie and TV screens; we have reason to criticize the artistic and theological effect of many crucifixes. They disaffect many people in regard to the real meaning of Christianity and the cross.

Originally, the early Christians never displayed the gruesome image of Christ on the cross. Their genuine belief and piety didn't allow them to concentrate on his agony. The crucifixion wasn't an altogether tragic event for them. They represented Christ royally triumphant alongside his cross. Or they bedecked the cross with jewels to let it glint with triumph. Without losing sight of suffering, they mixed the tragedy of sorrow with the joy of victory.

2. A theology of the cross

What brings this all to mind is the verse in John's gospel reading: "and the Son of Man must be lifted up as Moses lifted up the serpent in the desert, so that everyone who believes may have eternal life in him." The word "lifted up" has a very peculiar meaning wherever it occurs in his gospel (8:28, 12:32). It has a double meaning in John's mind—to be crucified and to be glorified. Jesus' dying on the cross is at once a crucifixion and a glorification. By climbing on the cross, apparently, he takes his first step of ascent to glory. The first step is followed by the resurrection, ascension, and enthronement in heaven. The cross is turned into a sign of victory.

John wasn't so naive as to think that anybody looking at the crucified Christ would become aware of victory. The victory was seen only by those who had faith in the Son of Man. The Son of Man title itself suggested to John how there must have been a descent before there could be an ascent. The upward movement began only after the downward movement was over. Just as the Hebrews were asked by Moses to look up at the serpent for healing, so the Hebrews of his day were to be healed of their sins by looking at Christ with faith. Faith was for them and is for us the gift of seeing Christ in a moment of triumph.

3. Medieval devotion

This beautiful and glorious faith-vision disappeared when, for centuries long, Christians paid more and more attention to the *human* Christ. There was nothing wrong, surely, with their belief in his humanity, but the attention grew out of all proportion to the reality. Christians developed devotions to his sacred wounds, his pierced heart, and his precious blood. The vision of the stigmatic Francis of Assisi fitted into this devotional life. Several such devotions continue into our own day.

We have no quarrel with the pendulum of piety so long as it doesn't swerve off an orthodox course. It must always keep in line with the truth of the Gospel. It goes wrong if it moves people to violence or stirs up their lust for blood, as can easily happen in a bloodthirsty western civilization.

4. Light and shadow

The truth about the cross is that it both sheds light and casts shadow upon life. Its beams, with the arms and legs of Christ outstretched upon them, cast the light of joy and the shadow of sorrow. The Christian life isn't modeled after Christ's unless it merges joy with sorrow. To prefer darkness to light is possible to evil-minded men. Lacking the faith that enlightens their minds to see that what Christ does is done in God, they miss the meaning of the cross.

John the evangelist places before us the vision of a cross covered over with light and shade. He suggests we see that cross here and now, not something out of the distant past nor a sign to appear in the far-off future. The cross flickers light and shadow, as if signaling for us to make a momentous decision. Do we or not believe in the light that is Christ? Do we accept or reject him? His coming into human life and death on the cross are an occasion for judgment. In making his decision for or against Christ man judges himself. Judgment isn't tomorrow or the day following but today, now.

5. Motivated by love

The faith-decision with which John confronts us, isn't a mere choice between light and darkness, joy and sorrow. John dangles before our eyes a motive we can hardly resist, the picture of a loving God, rich in mercy. "Yes, God loved the world so much that he gave his only Son, so that everyone who believes in him may not be lost but may have eternal life . . . so that through him the world might be saved." Faith alone can't accept the shadow of the cross, for it reminds one too much of the dark side of life. Faith is brightened with love.

Both faith and love are gifts from God, the tokens of "his goodness towards us in Christ Jesus." The cross then is a saving event in your life, though "not by anything that you have done, so that nobody can claim credit." Like the priceless art of a crucifix or crucifixion-painting, Christians are formed by the cross of Christ. "We are God's work of art, created in Christ Jesus to live the good life as from the beginning he had meant us to live it." The cross isn't merely a Christian symbol but our life.

Fifth Sunday of Lent
Jr 31:31-34; Heb 5:7-9; Jn 12:20-33

The Heart of Religion

1. Religious decline

Arnold Toynbee, the British historian, author of the twelve-volume history of civilization, who once maintained the only hope for the survival of western civilization was the rebirth of the Christian spirit, has changed his mind. Now an octogenarian, he no longer believes orthodox faith and religion will help the western world to survive. Should there be any ethical reform at all—a spiritual goal of life, simpler ways, and honesty among peoples—it will rise out of the spiritual needs of the contemporary western world.

Vatican II already observed in 1965, with alarm, the decline of the religious attitude and behavior among many peoples, and commented: "This split between the faith many profess and their daily lives deserves to be counted among the most serious errors of our age" (*Constitution on the Church in the Modern World*, #43). Professional and social activities can't be divorced from religion.

2. Man, a religious being

The source of religion is twofold: human needs and human response to the divine covenant with man. The first is a long, rocky, and uncertain journey; the second is the Judaeo-Christian way.

Religious belief and practice are rooted deeply in the reality of man. Man is not only a rational animal, as the Greek philosophers taught, but a religious animal too. Man naturally has a spirit of religion, a religious instinct. Religion in him lies at a deeper level than the level of thought or feeling, though at times it rises to the surface of thought or feeling. It expresses itself in prayer, worship, ethical human relationships. Whoever doesn't accede to his religious needs will suffer pangs worse than hunger or thirst. The issue of religion always faces man, who needs to know the meaning of life, of his activity, his death.

The religious desires and needs of man, if keen enough, are discoverable by man himself, as the history of religion shows, but it would be much easier and surer for him to accept the Judaeo-Christian tradition. This tradition is also rooted in the reality of man, with the additional merit of having been revealed by God. By substituting "religion" for the biblical term "covenant" we realize better what the common traits of religion are. Many facts turned up by researchers in ethnic or tribal religions are to be found in the Judaeo-Christian tradition.

3. Religion is free

Religion is a *free* attitude and practice. Freely coming from God, it doesn't coerce man. Even though God, by means of instilling religion in the heart of man, lets man know who is master, he doesn't enslave man. God covenanted with Israelite man on his own initiative: "Then I will be their God and they shall be my people." Religious man has rights and duties, freely rejected or freely accepted. This basic freedom in religion allows man to think he can arbitrarily accept or reject religion with impunity.

4. Personal, interior

Some religionists identify their religion with magic and superstition. They appeal to God only in time of trouble or need, a stopgap God, a trouble-shooter. Because of the contemporary decline in the religious attitude and practice, many can't depend too much upon the social and cohesive force of religion. Formerly, religion was felt to be more of a unifying force in family and society. Religion used to be a stronger family tradition; parents can't always rely upon their children following in their faith. Presently it demands more "a *personal* and explicit adherence of faith." This explains why many are achieving "a more vivid sense of God" (ibid., #7).

For Jeremiah and for Jesus the personal character of religion was very important yet not comparable to the interiorizing of religion. Religion must be written "on the hearts" of men, in the Jeremian sense, for this is what makes it "new." Jeremiah and Jesus lived an intense personal and interior religion. Jesus prayed "aloud and in *silent* tears." He "submitted so humbly that his prayer was heard." "He learnt to obey through suffering," and in turn "he became for all who obey him the source of eternal salvation."

True religion sets a priority upon the interior values of obedience, love, and the knowledge of God (faith). "For, of its very nature, the exercise of religion consists before all else in those internal, voluntary, and free acts whereby man sets the course of his life directly toward God" (*Declaration on Religious Freedom*, #3).

5. External, social

People who descry the external changes in the Church and liturgy—Latin to English, the use of folk and guitar music, the abolition of the Friday fast, Communion under both kinds, liturgical experiments, etc.—imply the necessity of externals in religion because of its social nature. "The social nature of man itself requires that he should give external expression of his internal acts of religion; that he should participate with others in matters religious; that he should profess his religion in community" (ibid.).

Religion expresses itself visibly, socially, institutionally.

The sacraments, preaching, priesthood, and worship are features of our faith which, if we didn't have them already, would have to be invented by our own religious ingenuity. Pertinent to human well-being, they help civilization to advance.

But the externals themselves won't help us out of the contemporary religious crisis. We need what Jeremiah was calling for in his day—a new heart for religion. The alternatives are to turn to the Asiatic religions or the invention of new religions, or to pump new blood into the heart of the old and established religions. Jeremiah demanded that the realization of the old religion begin *anew*. A little vigorous spiritual exercise can still stimulate the heart of religion.

Passion Sunday
Is 50:4-7; Ph 2:6-11; Mk 14:1-15:47

A Lonely Death

1. A Christian belief

"He suffered under Pontius Pilate, was crucified, died, and was buried." This is how the ancient Apostles' Creed formulates one of our beliefs. In one sense, it seems strange we should have to *believe* in the suffering, death, and burial of Christ. We don't ordinarily *believe* in anything of the kind. We know it to be a fact: every man must suffer, die, be buried, and since Christ was truly man, why should we believe in his fate? Why not just accept it as a historical fact, just as we know about the death, say, of Caesar, Anthony, or Cleopatra?

But belief in the suffering, death, and burial of Christ is something special. His is not only the case of an innocent man meeting up with a violent death. Nor is it one more number added to the list of capital punishment. His suffering and death involve us in mystery. He reveals the secret of suffering. The mystery of Jesus lies in his passion and death, although he spoke about it "quite openly" and prepared his disciples for it (Mk 8:32). Peter, who refused to hear about it, was told that his way of thinking was "not God's but man's" (Mk 8:33). In other words, God's way of looking at suffering and death is for us a matter of belief, not just a bit of factual knowledge. Faith alone sees best in the dark night of suffering and death.

2. Jesus suffering and dying

Jesus felt the full responsibility for and involvement in

his suffering and death. He was in no way anesthetized against them. "And a sudden fear came over him, and great distress." His soul was "sorrowful to the point of death." His disciples fell asleep while Jesus prayed. He "prayed that, if it were possible, this hour might pass him by." We can afford to be insensitive to a suffering and death that doesn't concern us; we can afford to fall asleep.

To Jesus, suffering and death were a task. He could have been relieved of this task, but that way out would have been an escape, not a destiny. He sought the help he needed for the accomplishment of his task. "Everything is possible for you," he prayed to his Father. "Take this cup away from me. But let it be as you, not I, would have it."

3. For punishment or fulfillment

To others, the suffering and death of Christ seemed like punishment, which they intended it to be. Both the Jewish leaders and the Roman authority connived and cooperated in making Jesus' suffering and death look like a well-deserved punishment. They brought two charges against him, blasphemy and political sedition, respectively. Jesus in the view of the Jewish leaders was a messianic pretender who sidestepped and subverted the Mosaic Law. For this pretension they accused him broadly of blasphemy—anyone who rejects any part of the Mosaic Law makes himself equal to God. To Pontius Pilate, the Roman authority, Jesus appeared to be a political upstart and threat. Thus he was accused and condemned for simultaneously divine and human pretensions.

The mystery of Jesus' suffering and death is complicated further by the fact that while he was judged and condemned and executed by human authority he was doing God's will. God willed that his Son fulfill the Old Testament prophecies and suffer the same fate as the prophets themselves. The third Servant song in Isaiah conveys this

idea and purpose: the Servant was to turn the other cheek.
We hear about the fulfillment of this purpose in the Philip-
pian hymn: "he was humbler yet, even to accepting death
on a cross."

The blood Christ spilled on the cross he "poured out
for many." The Father commanded him "to give life as a
ransom for many" (Mk 10:45). The suffering and death
Jesus bore for a double purpose—to complete the task as-
signed to him and to free mankind from sin. The one purpose interlinked with the other. The Lamb of God took
away the sins of the world.

4. To die alone

Despite the involvement of so many others in his suffering and death—the Jewish leaders, the Roman authority,
God himself, and mankind, Jesus suffered and died very
much alone. His was the loneliest of deaths. Where were
his disciples at the crucial moment? "They all deserted
him and ran away." Never before did he feel so empty and
lost. Even his heavenly Father didn't help him feel equal
to his task: "My God, my God, why have you deserted
me?"

The task of dying befalls every man, but no dying man
was so lonely as Jesus. He was the only man without guilt
before God, the innocent victim of the sin of the world.
Faith in the crucified Jesus isn't measured by what one
sees, the punishment of a rebel and blasphemer. Faith
penetrates into this cruel event and discovers there the
meaning of death. Neither Jew nor Roman was in command of Christ's death; Jesus let God rule in his life and
death.

5. The meaning

Suffering directs a man's attention inward, to himself.
Faith, on the contrary, directs his attention outward. Faith

in the crucified Christ teaches that no one since Christ need die alone. The dying and those awaiting death may look upon the Crucified and see in him the meaning of their own death. They're able to die with him and gain the same victory over death as he experienced.

Suffering and dying are harder for the doubtful and irresolute. The reason is that they have nothing to suffer and die for or no one to die with. The way of the cross is clear to the faithful alone. Men in pain who forget their relationship to God through Christ, become fearful of everything and everyone. Christian faith encourages man to suffer and die with *conviction*.

EASTER SEASON

Easter Sunday
Ac 10:34, 37-43; Col 3:1-4; Jn 20:1-9

We Better Believe It

You've heard, no doubt, about people dying of incurable diseases who have their bodies frozen and kept in deep freeze vaults. They want themselves preserved for the day a cure is found for their disease, when they will be brought back to life. Besides illustrating the fact that this life has its limits, they harbor the hope for immortality. They experience too soon for their own satisfaction that this life is incomplete. The recognition of life's limits raises the question of something beyond.

1. Christian death

Death for the Christian is a kind of frontier, the Christian himself is a frontiersman who knows his limits. Death makes him aware of his limits but prompts him to ask what lies beyond. Death itself doesn't unlock the secret of life, for that secret surpasses all present-day knowledge. As Christian death leads to the resurrection, so Christian faith goes beyond the limits of knowledge.

The resurrection—we better believe it in view of a life uncramped by time-space limits. The resurrection faith helps us to a fuller meaning of life and to a better understanding of man. But, to begin with, the resurrection was a real Easter event that happened within time-space limits. The resurrection is real too because originally it broke out of such limits.

2. Empty tomb

The gospels situate the resurrection event within time: they mention what will happen "after three days" or what takes place on "the first day of the week." The resurrection event sets a decisive date in the history of mankind, a turning point, when God in Christ rules over death. Moreover, to clear away every evidence of death, he leaves behind no mortal remains—an empty tomb. Immediately the people who want to discredit the fact of the resurrection, resort to the conflicting stories that the disciples stole the body, or that the gardener took it away.

The first to witness the empty tomb were women, particularly Mary of Magdala. The Johannine gospel relates how she found the tomb empty, and afterwards how the risen Christ appeared to her. Both the appearance and the empty tomb gave the women reason to witness to the resurrection. They ran off to tell the apostles. A curious fact, this, because women had no official status as witnesses in Jewish law. This didn't keep the apostles from trusting them. They came running to see for themselves. Our belief in the resurrection is assured by the reliability of these witnesses—Paul, Mary Magdalene, Peter, John, and others.

3. Witness

Our faith, then, is tied to a long chain of witnesses. First of all to Christ, the first link in the chain. He bears witness to God the Father who puts his stamp of approval upon the life of Jesus by raising him from the dead. The women come to the tomb to pay respects to Christ and find the tomb empty. They report the fact to the apostles. And the apostles hand down a tradition in which we still believe. The keeping of such a tradition evidences the power of the resurrection.

The Christian faith today is examined by non-Christians in the same way that the first followers of Christ looked into his resurrection. They had to have a witness of the risen Christ, without which the Christian faith would have floundered from the first. So today, wherever and whenever we live the Christian faith, we testify to a resurrection that took place in the past but is operative in the present. Non-Christians will more easily believe in us the more reliable or genuine our witness is.

4. Resurrection faith and life

Resurrection faith develops and grows like the Easter lily. The Easter lily takes its start from the form of a seed, the seed evolves into a bulb, the bulb shoots forth stems, buds edge forth from the stems, and the buds flower into the lily-white petals with their faint but pervasive fragrance. The resurrection faith begins with the risen Jesus, he is first witnessed by his disciples, they pass along a tradition, that tradition bears fruit in our lives, and we live in the hope of seeing it flower throughout the whole world of men. The resurrection is their destiny as well as ours, hence we have to do our part in making it believable for them.

Though the resurrection event is linked with facts of time and space, its power is unlimited. "Jesus has risen"— that means he has scored a victory over death, over sin which is a cause of death, and over satan who is an instigator of sin. His victory, being eternal, is ever-present in our overcoming sinful habits and beginning anew. Jesus didn't rise and leave an empty tomb so that we can mark this event down on the calendar as simply one that took place behind our backs or before we were born. His resurrection was an ascent into a new life which crops out into our own.

Christ is our new life. He reveals us to ourselves, what our life will be like once the reality of the end-time breaks into it. The resurrection is a radical transformation into a new life, and Jesus is the first fruit of this transformation. Through the resurrection Jesus was shown to be God's Son. We'll be shown to be sons of God in the same way. His resurrection is our guarantee of union with him in the family of God. Jesus anticipates what will happen to us. We better believe it, or we'll never experience what God has in store for us—our full humanity, our complete life.

Second Sunday of Easter
Ac 4:32-35; 1 Jn 5:1-6; Jn 20:19-31

Communal Living

1. Communes

A newspaper headline read in part, "More Affluent Adults Quit Corporate World To Lead Simpler Lives." You may have seen similar reports about people here and abroad joining city or county communes, getting away from the materialistic and individualistic way of life. Communes have been mushrooming throughout the land. Estimates of their number run from 2,000 to 3,000. Hundreds of thousands have lived in them, for shorter or longer stays. Their membership is predicted to run into the millions, and communal living to be the wave of the future.

2. Christian communities

The communes with a Christian purpose hark back to the early Christian community ideally described in the Acts of the Apostles. St. Luke simply pictured what he saw: people united in the Christian faith and living together not necessarily under the same roof but sharing all things in common, while others sold their possessions and distributed their wealth to the needy. Early Christianity was lived in such communities. Christians had a feel for community. Their faith was bigger than themselves, individually, and so they gave to others, considering them more important than themselves.

Call this communism if you like. It was a healthy type which had for its model the life-style of Christ himself, who gathered men and women around him into a company of followers. They left their homes to share together, lived, prayed, ate, slept, traveled, labored together.

Many Christian communities, like the one centered around Christ, grew up as converts increased in number. They were all united on a voluntary and at first unsystematic basis. The one described in Acts had two principles regarding poverty. The possessions were held in common, and wealthy individuals sold their property and distributed their wealth among the poor. The idea of surrendering property was to make themselves equal in the Lord. Barnabas and the couple Ananias and Sapphira did so. The latter reneged on their earlier promise and were punished for it. Nor did all the early communities live up to their ideal. St. Paul puts his finger on their problems of divisiveness, selfishness, greediness, quarreling, and deceitfulness.

Communal living existed before Christ adapted it to the commandment of love. And communes existed long before the modern movement toward them. One of the longer-lasting and better known is the Catholic Worker Movement originated by Peter Maurin and Dorothy Day. It will serve for an illustration.

3. An example

The septuagenarian Dorothy Day still gives loyal and humble leadership to the Catholic Worker Movement. For 50 years she has worked among and served the broke and broken in the New York bowery. She lives among the poor as the woman of the poor, personally providing them with food, clothing, and shelter. She makes her home in the slums in order to serve the city's forgotten and lonely.

Her works of mercy are supported in many ways, one of which is the farming commune which raises much of the foodstuff fed to the poor. The daily struggle of living and sharing with the poor is neither an escapist nor a romantic way of life. Only those who have a religious dedication, who are filled with love and the spirit of sacrifice, can take it. Others can't stand the routine and discipline.

Dorothy Day and her Catholic Worker Movement weather the storms that inevitably hit communities, especially the lack of leadership and the individualistic spirit. The easiest way for any community to fail is for each member to go his own way, to do his own thing. Then goodwill departs from the community, and the community dies out. The same is true of every form of communal living.

Dorothy Day believes that tyranny and injustice which impoverish people must be fought by spiritual weapons, by non-violence and non-cooperation. She tries to live and work among the poor in accordance with the Sermon on the Mount which is summed up in the commandment of love. Critics find fault with her because she bucks the profit and interest system and stands for peace everywhere. She defends her movement: "People who take a materialistic view of human service wish to make a profit but we are trying to do our duty by our service without wages to our brothers."

4. Love for the common good

The Catholic Worker Movement, I think, comes very close to the model of the early Christian community. The original community shared the new life of the Christian, each member giving himself to the other. It committed itself to the love that knits people into unity. Everybody contributed to the common good. They were drawn together and gave testimony of their unity.

Genuine Christian communal living, whether it takes the form of a commune or not, is here to stay. The Christian life has an inner force which gathers people into community. Love is that unifying force.

Genuine Christian communal living pricks the conscience of those who keep others poor by their selfish exploits and dishonest interests. It reacts to that unjust distribution of goods in today's world, where not enough property is held in common and too much wealth is in the hands of a few.

Genuine Christian communal living is a sign of our times, a positive sign of fellowship in Christ whereby people are seen as brothers and sisters of his, and a negative sign of protest against that accumulation of wealth, fat consumption, which does more harm than good among peoples.

Third Sunday of Easter
Ac 3:13-15, 17-19; 1 Jn 2:1-5; Lk 24:35-48

Understanding Scripture

1. The risen Jesus speaks

The readings from Acts and Luke, inverted, make for a better understanding of our liturgy today. Both written by Luke, first the gospel, then the Acts, they were meant to dovetail. Set the address by the apostle Peter alongside the gospel, and note the parallel at once. Jesus explained himself and the last events of his life by reference to the Old Testament, especially the prophets. Peter did the same. Jesus ended his instructions with "You are witnesses to this," while Peter added, "and to that fact we are the witnesses."

2. Fearful and dumbfounded

The apostles were alarmed and frightened by their first encounter with the risen Christ. They thought they saw a ghost. Christ wanted to prove to them he was more than a vision, that he was for real. He appealed to their senses of sight, touch, hearing. And then he did a surprising thing: he ate a piece of grilled fish. When you think this over, you begin to wonder about it. Is it possible for a risen body to eat? If so, will our spiritual bodies (ours after our resurrection) be able to eat too? Will they *need* nourishment? Such questions must be left unanswered. We can speculate or theorize about them without arriving at any indisputable conclusions. They arouse our curiosity about the afterlife.

A second aspect of this Easter encounter merits more of our attention because it has practical consequences for us. Among the several ways in which Jesus tried to impress his followers with his risen but real appearance, he had to overcome their fear. Indeed they felt fear from two sources —from the hostile Jews who saw in them a threat to the old-time religion and accused them of stealing Jesus' body, and from the unexpected sight of the resurrected Christ. He calmed their doubts and fears with the greeting, "Peace be with you."

The disciples supposedly should have been ready to recognize Christ at once, having lived with him so intimately so long. No, they were dumbfounded by his resurrection life and disinclined to believe the early reports about him. It took more than his appearance and his empty tomb to bring them around to belief in him. More than an appeal to their senses to convince them. He had to explain how his life, death, and resurrection fulfilled the Old Testament expectations of the Messiah. "He then opened their minds to understand the scriptures. . ."

3. The Old Testament

We must remember that the only scriptures available at that time were the Old Testament, which contained three principal types of writing: history, prophecy, and wisdom literature. The disciples were familiar with it, though not to the extent Christ was. Reading the Old Testament was one variety of religious experience for them; the interpretation Jesus gave to it was another.

Sometimes, and then not altogether correctly, the Old Testament is taught as a document of fear and the New Testament as one of love. This distinction is too neat and facile. The Old Testament neither abrogates love—the Ten Commandments summed up in love are to be found there, nor does the New Testament abrogate fear. Both offer a blend of fear and love, two varieties of religious experience. The disciples had to banish their fear before lovingly identifying their former Master.

The Old Testament, once so helpful in understanding Christ, is still an aid to faith. It teaches an incomparably valuable knowledge of God and man, the ways in which God deals with men. Some things are "incomplete and temporary" in it, and as a result they have only historical value. But for the most part it expresses a lively sense of God, offers wisdom about human life, contains a wonderful treasury of prayers, particularly the psalms, and reveals gradually the mystery of salvation (cf. *Constitution on Divine Revelation,* #15).

The New Testament contains the teaching and life of Jesus to the extent it was recalled by the Church and her writers and inspired by the Holy Spirit. Jesus himself relied upon the Old Testament in clarifying himself to the befuddled disciples. That he saw himself against the Old Testament background is unquestionable. I recall a statement by a rabbi, a friend and colleague, several weeks before his death. He told me he was a Jewish believer, because he recognized so much of his own religion in the Jewish Jesus, accepted all that Jesus taught.

4. Growth in understanding

We Christians who are entrusted with the entire Bible, should grow in the understanding of it. God is its author and the author of our faith. Our faith will grow correspondingly with our understanding of the scriptures. We share with the disciples their fear and dumbfoundedness. For both of us, as St. Jerome says in his classic statement, "Ignorance of the scriptures is ignorance of Christ."

The scriptures are more easily available to us than they were to the disciples. The Bible has become a best-seller. Our missalettes are so handy that with their use we can both hear and read the word of God, bringing to bear several senses upon it. Our worship therefore is instructional. "For in the liturgy God speaks to his people and Christ is proclaiming his gospel" (*Constitution on the Sacred Liturgy*, #33).

Scriptural reading won't help us spiritually unless we accompany it with prayer. In the two combined God and man talk together. St. Ambrose wrote about this combination: "We speak to him when we pray; we hear him when we read the divine sayings."

Fourth Sunday of Easter
Ac 4:8-12; 1 Jn 3:1-2; Jn 10:11-18

Christian Leadership

1. Crisis in authority

The polls show, and experience bears out, a crisis in authority. People are losing confidence in their leaders, both Church and civic. A typical complaint reads, "Everywhere people tell me how helpless they feel to make their own thoughts and will felt by their leaders." They are unable to get through the bureaucratic channels to their public officials, their union bosses, management, hierarchy. The leaders are insulated from the common man.

2. Crisis in obedience

In all fairness, we should look at the constituency too. If trust in leadership is dwindling, what about the followers—do they measure up in loyalty? There's the rub. People just don't cry out against bad leadership; some simply don't want to be led or ruled. They oppose the democratic spirit to the bureaucratic system. They hold that power belongs to the people. The mood of the times is for everybody to do his own thing, to assert his right to freedom. A shepherd is pretty much at a loss with an obstreperous sheep. Needless to say, good leadership requires good followers.

The first and third readings present a similar situation in the time of Christ and the early Church. The only difference is that the two lived in an agricultural society, we in an industrial; hence they spoke of leadership in terms of a shepherd tending his flock. The shepherd figure is someone most of us know only by hearsay; very few ever met a shepherd personally.

3. Peter speaks up

When Peter rose to speak in defense of faith in Christ, tried, tortured, killed, and risen from the dead, he and his group were under arrest. He was a spokesman for the rest before the Sanhedrin, the ruling class of the Jewish religion. Once before, the night his Master was on trial, Peter had a chance to confess his faith and failed to do so. This time he vindicated himself, manifesting a quality of true leadership—fortitude.

Behind Peter at this moment of his own trial we must see standing, though invisible, the figure of Christ. For Christ is the *real* authority in the Church, however invisibly he exercises it in the persons appointed or elected. His saying, "I am the good shepherd," means that he's the *true* leader, without equal. His qualifications for leadership are twofold.

4. Good leadership

First and foremost Christ is a rugged leader. Pictures of the Good Shepherd dripping with sentimentality falsify his real role. He's a loving shepherd, giving tender care to his sheep, but his goodness is evidenced especially by his laying down his life for his sheep. A good shepherd was promised of old (Ez 37:24) who would guard his sheep at the risk of his life (1 S 17:34f., Is 31:4). Good leadership started in Hebrew tradition with the fidelity of God to his people. Henceforward they could test the quality of their human leaders by this criterion. They continued to chant the psalm verse, "Yahweh is my shepherd, I lack nothing" (Ps 23:1).

Secondly, Christ is so much with his sheep that they are known to him as he to them. He hears the bleat of their needs, and they recognize his voice of command. Openness between the two makes for a mutually helpful knowledge. To have leaders so eminent as to be unavailable and unserviceable doesn't seem right. People grow tired of grand, spectacular showmanship. They resent the high-handed way they are dealt with. The remark by Christ about "hired hands" wasn't just a shot in the dark but was directed toward the autocratic Pharisees.

Leadership in the Church and in civil society differ in at least one major respect. Church leadership is a charism, a gift from Christ no Church leader, not even the pope, can claim as his own. Popes, bishops, priests, laypeople have their leadership in trusteeship from God. He entrusts it to whomever he pleases, with the proviso that it be used for the spiritual good of his people. Nobody can fundamentally qualify for it. The charism of leadership doesn't necessarily enhance the personality of its possessor or make him holier. He's held accountable for the use of this charism. True leaders command respect and obedience through experience, knowhow, careful work, a sense of responsibility to God and to their people, and devotion to their task.

5. What to expect from it

We mustn't expect our leaders to tell us always what we like to hear. Sometimes they have to guide us along difficult paths. Incapable of doing the whole job of following Christ by themselves, they ask us to do our best, to make sacrifices for the common good. Their duty is to encourage but not cater to us, and to correct the recreant.

We shouldn't expect our leaders to be without fault. Yet Christ promised to be with his Church, to guarantee her against fatal error and to keep her from failing completely. He will see to it that she attains her proper goal—salvation. The Church is willing to acknowledge mistakes of the past, and realizes we still need divine guidance and help.

The critic who shouts loudest about poor leadership in the Church isn't always an outstanding example of either leadership or obedience. To be misguided by oneself is far worse than to be led poorly by others, for in the former case leadership is taken into one's own hands. God may not be able to change such a one and guide him right.

In this crisis of authority, we still have confidence that Christ leads us invisibly, and that whatever he does through his foremen, at local levels, can heal and save. Peter acting in Jesus' name healed an adult man.

Fifth Sunday of Easter
Ac 9:26-31; 1 Jn 3:18-24; Jn 15:1-8

Conscience

1. What is it?

"Let your conscience be your guide." This statement (a song title too) is true as far as it goes. Its full truth needs explanation. Were every man to listen to the dictates of his conscience in any and every situation, without further ado, without regard for any other standard or norm, society would be in shambles. Other factors have to be considered along with this statement, such as whether your conscience is correct, whether your conscience has sought for the truth, and whether it accepts objective standards or norms.

Listen to what Vatican II wrote on the conscience: "In the depths of conscience, man detects a law which he does not impose on himself, but which holds him to obedience. Always summoning him to love good and avoid evil, the voice of conscience can when necessary speak to his heart more specifically: do this, shun that. For man has in his heart a law written by God. To obey it is the very dignity of man; according to it he will be judged" (*Constitution on the Church in the Modern World*, #16).

Conscience always "tells it like it is?" Definitely not. At times it fouls people up, gets them into bad straits, because they don't really listen to their conscience but to their feelings or emotions or to a "voice-within-themselves," whatever that may mean. Conscience is a value-judgment, an act of the human *mind* deciding what's right or wrong for us to do. Human acts generally are either virtuous or sinful, and the mind can approve or disapprove of them. Through his conscience man bears the responsibility for his acts.

2. Of many kinds

One word in the second reading today lends itself to various translations depending on its context. The Hebrew word for "heart" may also signify conscience. The Jerusalem Bible translates "conscience" here rather than "heart." Heart in the original Hebrew is man's whole conscious, intelligent, and free personality. In one sense it's the *whole man,* as if the Hebrew were to say of a man, "He's all heart." Man, as St. John writes in his first letter, stands accused or acquitted in God's presence according to his conscience. The man who conscientiously keeps God's commandments has God living in him and himself living in God. His conscience, if nourished with the divine commandments, especially that of love, is bound to bear fruit in a good life. It will produce acts of virtue rather than of vice. It will make a man of him.

Conscience, being an act of the mind, needs to be *taught.* All sorts of consciences exist among people, which accounts for judgments differing much over social issues. One conscience may be good and sound, another clear, another weak, and still another mistaken. You can almost have your pick of consciences. Some try to circumvent or avoid their consciences, others try to deceive them. In each and every case the conscience has need for education and practice. Or else it grows dull or lax and easily slips into error. Only when the conscience is operating in good order can we say that the final decision for human acts rests with it.

3. No law unto itself

The thing to remember is that no man can judge rightly

without standards or norms. The Christian conscience has, all in all, three such norms. Sometimes the conscience gets balled up by not keeping norms in the order of their importance, by not putting first things first. The law of God comes first, a basic norm no man can flaunt without diminishing his manhood. God set this law up within the very nature of man, for man's own good. By means of his conscience man sees and acknowledges this law within himself, and becomes the happier for observing it.

A second set of laws is laid down by the Church. They outline the duty of our relationship to God and to fellow Christians. In the formation of his conscience the Catholic ought to attend to the doctrine and law of his Church. Since in some cases both are subject to change, the duty of his conscience is to keep himself well-informed and observant of them.

The Christian who wants to keep his conscience pure and upright has a third outside source of help, but one subtler than the other two. He must be attuned to the inspiration of the Holy Spirit. Christ promised his Church that delicate guidance of his Spirit which makes her members wiser than all human judgments.

4. States of conscience

Far be it from us to cast human consciences into molds, but we can discern three states of conscience among people. The first is the state of the pure conscience, simple and sincere. Its voice echoes in the purity of the human heart. The law of Christ is so assimilated into the heart that, if the heart be yours, "Love and do as you will" (St. Augustine). The opposite of the pure, delicate conscience is the tainted, lax conscience "which by degrees grows practically sightless as a result of habitual sin" (ibid.). The average Christian conscience, however, is in some stage of incomplete development, adult in years but more or less infantile or adolescent in judgment. Due to past failures, opportunities lost because of weakness or cowardice, it hasn't developed sufficiently.

Happily for us, God is greater than our consciences and sees into our hearts. He can't live our lives for us, nor can he substitute his own wise judgment for our consciences.He won't pronounce us guilty if,after having made judgments or decisions in good faith, we find ourselves in the wrong. We won't be afraid in his presence.

Sixth Sunday of Easter
Ac 10:25-26, 34-35, 44-48; 1 Jn 4:7-10; Jn 15:9-17

No Greater Love

Miss America, in an interview, said she learned of the love of God through a friend."My friend made me understand Christ. I had a new understanding of my fellow man. Most of all I had a new understanding of myself." This acknowledgement by a beauty contest winner says much about the value of friendship that accords with scriptural teaching.

1. Friendship with Christ

A part of that teaching we just heard from the letter and gospel of John, whose writings are replete with the language of love. Hardly any other New Testament writing, excepting perhaps 1 Corinthians 13, compares with his on the subject of love and friendship. It seems as if "the disciple Jesus loved" (Jn 13:23) has to reciprocate the love of Christ for himself with an expression of love that sounds almost lyrical. Since love is the activity most essential to and characteristic of God, and love flows from God through Christ, John sees the source of his love in God. Christ said, "As the Father has loved me, so I have loved you," and John could have responded later that this is why he wrote a gospel of love.

Christ, in claiming and calling his disciples friends, was finishing his life with them with a gesture of love—a friendship meal. He had taken many meals with them, but never this way. When he first assembled the community, it was only a loosely-connected group without many ties of friendship. Gradually he became the focal point of a growing community of friends. He was willing to give himself unconditionally to the requirements of friendship: "A man can have no greater love than to lay down his life for his friends." Christ sealed his friendship with the gift of his death.

What would have happened to his little community had Christ not bound them together with his everlasting friendship? As a matter of fact, after his death they dispersed. They gathered again once he reappeared among them.

2. Genuine friends

Members of a family, a community, a society, can live and work together without forming friendships. A community is not unlikely to have a degree of solidarity but lack friendship. They may live and work *alongside* one another. A common goal may unite a group for a while, yet no one can count a single friend among the others. Christian friendship is more than a getting along together or a doing something socially. "A genuine friendship," wrote St. Jerome in a letter to a friend, "necessarily is cemented by the glue of Christ. It does not depend on material considerations, or on the actual physical presence of the two people, or on shrewd, weedling flattery" (*The Satirical Letters*, p. 152).

Although Christ was eventually to disappear from their physical view, his friends retained him spiritually in their midst. We have some indication, particularly in 3 John 15, that his early followers were called by the title of "friends." They retained the unifying force of his Spirit, who is the Bond of love.

3. A thing divine

The love of God adds something special to friendship which allows no substitute. Friendships can and do exist on a purely human level where kindliness and love join the two people together. Yet even the classic Latin author Cicero, who had no explicit knowledge of Holy Scripture, defined friendship as "the agreement on things human *and divine,* joined with kindliness and love." Writing to a friend of his, St. Augustine comments on this definition: "Thus it happens that there can be no full and true agreement about things human among friends who disagree about things divine, for it necessarily follows that he who despises things divine esteems things human otherwise than as he should, and that whoever does not love Him who made man has not learned to love man aright" (Letter 258).

The agreement between this comment and the interview with the beauty contest winner is remarkable. Neither of the two, Augustine or Miss America, could see themselves truly and fully understanding and loving a friend without divine help. Christ had to be the mediator of their friendship. The love of friendship is *revealed* by him and *perceived* by men and women of faith.

4. Sharing together

Friendship requires reciprocity, mutuality. This mutuality or reciprocity is supreme if what friends have to share is spiritual. The spiritual is sharable without suffering any diminution. Persons willing to share Christ not only experience no loss but enrich their common life with him. This is what makes friendships, as distinct from sexual involvements, so precious and fruitful. The history of Christianity is full of examples of saints who shared the life of Christ: Christ and John the Apostle, John Chrysostom and Basil, Benedict and Scholastica, Francis of Assisi and Clare, Theresa of Avila and John of the Cross, Francis de Sales and Jane Frances de Chantal. Some of the examples prove that men and women can become fast friends without falling into sinful sex.

5. The supreme love

The rest of us don't measure up to the love Christ has for us. Our love approaches his by degrees. Many don't want to go beyond the degree of love they feel comfortable with. They can live with it and don't want to be challenged and engaged further. They reach the point where friendship falls short.

God's love plays no favorites. In Christ he shows no partiality, no discrimination between friend and enemy. We're drawn to or away from him by those interpersonal relationships which we find friendly or unfriendly.

Solemnity of the Ascension
Ac 1:1-11; Ep 1:17-23; Mk 16:15-20

Infinitely Great

1. Beyond the cloud

Christ "ascended into heaven and is seated at the right hand of the Father." He re-assumed the position of power and glory he had before becoming man. The glorious ascension is an event we believe, profess after this homily, but don't quite understand. The real ascension is invisible to us. Its meaning will come to us only after we've joined Christ in his triumph.

Christ's spiritual ascent into heaven contrasts with satan's descent or fall from similar heights of power and glory. Christ said he saw satan fall "like lightning from heaven" (Lk 10:18). Satan descended from heaven; Jesus ascended there. When satan fell from his lofty post, leaving heaven with his company of evil spirits, in a sort of defiant gesture toward God he determined to drag mankind along with him. Conquered by God in the heavenly sphere, he's set upon conquering man in the earthly. If satan hates any liturgical celebration, it must be the Ascension because it commemorates Christ's final triumph over him.

2. The battle with satan

The evangelist Mark begins his narrative of Jesus' public life with the battle against satan (Mk 1:13) and ends it with Jesus' last instruction to his apostles to give satan the bounce in Jesus' name. Jesus' awareness of satan isn't simply peculiar to his time, for satan is accountable for many evil happenings. He and the enemies of Christ are as thick as thieves. Jesus has no doubt that satan is working behind the scenes to upset the plan of salvation.

Their battle over man rages continually. The big stick Jesus wields against the evil one is his miraculous power. By means of his miracles Jesus routs the demons and establishes his kingdom. So often does he resort to miracles, not only in banishing the evil spirits but in curing sickness, that his enemies accuse him of being in collusion with the devil. What a strange accusation—Jesus in collaboration with satan in the very means he uses against him.

3. The power and the glory

The scene of the ascension is noteworthy as the same scene where Jesus experiences his deepest sorrow. Mt. Olivet is at once the summit of his sorrow and the summit of his joy. From there he takes his departure for his heavenly home. The death, resurrection, and ascension are a series of acts concluding his victory over death, sin, and satan, and prefacing his glorification. As he disappears from human view, he is enthroned in glory at the right hand of his Father. He arrives at his full glory only at his enthronement. Fittingly, then, the liturgy speaks of his "glorious" ascension.

The kingdom of God established on earth, Jesus reigns "Most High" "in the glory of God the Father." At his triumphal entry into heaven he becomes in his humanity "the ruler of everything" who accomplishes the humanly impossible task of liberating man from every evil. His power and glory are supreme. He rules over the rebellious spirits too. The All-powerful, he brooks no human or superhuman interference. Where his power is the greatest, invincible, his glory shines the fullest.

4. Dim victory

The fact that our Lord and Savior is unconquerable

should make us confident of victory, give us a sense of triumph. Does it really? Perhaps we have a small taste of victory, but the total victory is dimmed for us because of two reasons.

First, the continued presence of evil in our world. If our ascension is guaranteed, why should we have to struggle so hard against evil? Against satan? By getting rid of evil, permanently, Christ shows his power more gloriously. But then he would have to use his full power against our wills. He would have to bend them forcefully, compel us to do good. Truthfully, do we want him to do that since we're so much in love with our freedom? We can't have both in our present life-trial—invincible force and unlimited freedom.

Secondly, the doctrine of satan and a descent into hell are uncongenial to us. With an unsteady spirit of faith, we can't easily envision the almighty power of Christ or, contrariwise, the ferocity of the devil's attack. Satan is made to look silly, stupid, grotesque. How little we realize that he's a cunning devil, the father of lies. The prevalence of satanism and devil worship in our society is symptomatic of his deceitful ways. His ways are usually the cloak-and-dagger kind. He likes nothing better than to have himself explained away psychologically.

5. At the foothills of heaven

Fortunately, the ascension hasn't taken Christ entirely out of this world. For the man who believes, loves, obeys, has a share already in Christ's power and scores a victory over satan, establishing the kingdom of God within himself. He rises above temptations, faults, sins. The grace of the ascension is his, the effect of a promise. "How infinitely great is the power that he (Christ) has exercised for us believers . . . these are the signs that will be associated with believers . . . the Lord working with them and confirming the word by the signs that accompanied it."

Christ ascended into heaven is the basis of our hope; he "was taken up to heaven . . . to claim for us a share in his divine life" (Preface of the Ascension). Nothing can harm us provided we rely upon his power, not even the whole kingdom of evil. We're members of his body, which means we already have one foot in heaven. This guarantee shouldn't lead us to a daredevil attitude. We join with you in the prayer, "May our minds dwell always on this heavenly home," the goal of the ascension.

Seventh Sunday of Easter
Ac 1:15-17, 20-26; 1 Jn 4:11-16; Jn 17:11-19

Faith and Love

1. Love

The theme of love is so exploited in popular art, music, and literature, that it should be easily recognized for what it is. But is it? Too often love is identified with emotion, passion, sex. People are fooled by love more often than by any other human quality. It doesn't come as a surprise, then, that a drama critic and columnist should write, "If you want to learn what love is, that's where to go"—the Bible. He gave this advice because the Bible is the original place where real, genuine, godlike, Christian love is taught.

Psychological and sociological studies of love and love-making proliferate. One would think they should be able to teach the true meaning and practice of love. But do they? They all fail at one point. Love of its essence isn't measurable, has no frontiers, no limits to which it can or should go. Authentic love comes from God who is eternal and infinite, and returns to him. God, the origin and end of love, is himself Love, always and everywhere diffusive of himself, outpouring his love.

2. Divine love

What makes divine love so real and distinctive is that it must be *believed*. Faith differentiates our outlook upon the world and its people. How do you regard it? Does it look like a loveless world? Or lovely and love-filled? Faith sheds a new light upon things, persons. Through faith we are enabled to see how the world is uniquely good. We need faith in ourselves, to know and accept ourselves. It takes the same faith to go out to others and see them as the beloved children of God. Faith assumes a divine viewpoint. We may have the best will in the world to discover and satisfy the deepest needs of others, but unless we have faith in them their needs won't reveal themselves. "Hence men can no longer love each other without God" (Hans Urs von Balthasar, *The God Question and Modern Man,* p. 143).

From the Bible emerge persons who portray faith and love for us. We encounter two in the biblical readings today.

3. John and Judas

John the apostle and evangelist comes first. He was close, very close to the heart of love, privileged to lean upon that heart at the Last Supper. Although love was the theme of all his writing, he would be the last to tell us he had only an understanding of divine love. "We ourselves have known and *put our faith* in God's love towards ourselves." As near as he was to Love Incarnate, he still had to believe in him. Without this belief, his love would have stopped short at the man Jesus. He would have had only a human love for Jesus, not divine. John loved God through Jesus, just as the Father loved John through his Son. Love attained its meeting-point in Jesus.

A second biblical figure, again one of Jesus' companions, is the betrayer Judas. Not as privileged as John was, but entrusted with a position of responsibility, Judas was the holder of the common purse. His engrossment with money and its value seems to have been his downfall. When Mary Magdalene bathed Jesus with a precious ointment, Judas complained it was a waste. It could have been sold and the money given to the poor. Was he really so concerned about the poor, or was his greed speaking out?

Why should Judas have fallen out of love for Jesus? He too was called by Christ to be of his select company. At the very moment of betrayal, Jesus expressed friendship for him. Judas nonetheless "chose to be lost." Choice is an

act of the will. Every virtue, faith included, is an act of
the will and, through repetition, becomes a habit of the
will. Judas seemed to lack that habit of faith in Christ
which alone supports divine love. Faith alone would have
let him see the love God has especially for the poor and
the needy.

Notwithstanding Judas' loss of faith in Christ, Christ
loved him to the end. His case is easier to explain if Jesus
had withdrawn his love. God never withdraws his love.
As faith in him weakens, it pulls away from his love. Love
"is always ready to trust" (1 Cor 13:6).

4. Faith in the love of God

Jesus' love for his companions was more than a mutual
human love. He conveyed an experience of the Father's
love to those who believed in him. Christian love cannot
but come from God, for *that* love must be *believed.*

Not only did Jesus love Judas with the love of God but
he demanded that the apostles love him in the same way.
He would have pointed to Judas as one who above all
needed to be loved.

Faith is a new sort of vision whereby we see Christ in
every man, woman, child, friend and enemy. Someone
may say, "I want to be loved for myself." Such a love is
possible—we can love others for themselves, but not *only*
for themselves if our love is to be Christian.

Christ asks us to see him in the hungry, thirsty, naked,
homeless, sick, imprisoned. To love the poor and needy for
themselves is a noble humanitarianism. Christ was more
than human, the mystery of Love Incarnate. Christian love
involves us in his mystery. "Hence it is not necessary, indeed not even possible, that Christian love should understand whence it comes and whither it goes" (Balthasar,
p. 148).

Faith says to love: "Interlaced we do well, but apart
we die. So it is not you without me, nor I without you."

Pentecost Sunday
Ac 2:1-11; 1 Cor 12:3-7, 12-13; Jn 20:19-23

Gift of the Spirit

1. A farewell gift

After having visited and been a guest of the human family, Christ left a farewell gift. On hearing this, you may immediately think of the Eucharist. It too was a farewell gift, but not what I have in mind. I refer to the gift of the Spirit, the Holy Spirit. All three readings record and give witness to a genuine experience of the risen Christ and the coming of the Holy Spirit. The Eucharist is a gift of 'inestimable value, no doubt, yet it too depends upon the Spirit, the gift of Christ to his Church. Not even his various gifts are as precious as the Spirit himself. He and they together have but one purpose—to benefit the Church.

The reception of the gift of the Spirit in the early Church was itself a remarkable event. The sights and sounds on that occasion, and the response to them, were all indications of a divine visit. God who visits man ensures getting through to man by telltale signs, as he did to Moses and Elijah (Ex 19:16-18; 1 K 19:11-12). So at Pentecost "the marvels of God"—wind, sound, fury, and fire—bewildered, amazed, and astonished the group of disciples. Christ's farewell gift, with its accompanying signs, left them ecstatic, which literally means "beside themselves." They never dreamt themselves capable of what the Spirit prompted them to do. They were changed men.

2. The Spirit in Catholic life

None of us is as shaken by Pentecost as the disciples were, nor can we be. The best we can do is to participate in this solemnity wholeheartedly and remain open to the inspiration and guidance of the Spirit. We Catholics, I think, have taken the Holy Spirit more or less for granted in the Church. Contacts with Protestants and especially Quakers have left me with an admiration of their reliance upon the Spirit. Much of their prayer implores him, and their theology of the Spirit is well developed.

What is the significance of the gift of the Spirit? The gift of the Spirit is the "law" of the new covenant. As God gave Moses the tablets of the Law on Mt. Sinai, so Christ gave the "law" of the Spirit in fulfillment of a promise. The Spirit isn't concentrated in Christ, the Head of the Church, but diffused through his body. He who dwells in us ought to be our law. Not that he replaces the commandments or substitutes for the law of love. He interiorizes that law in our hearts, makes it the spirit of our life, work, and worship. He fills us with the love to do God's will.

God's will intends us principally to speak for Jesus our Lord, and witness to him by our life and action, which we do "under the influence of the Holy Spirit." The Spirit is the decisive and driving force in the proclamation of Christ's message. He inaugurates the era of the Church and her mission. Without his power and aid, our words would fall flat upon deaf ears and our witness would be a lie. The Spirit is, as Christ himself (1 Jn 2:1), our advocate, that is, our intercessor and support.

3. His unifying role

The law of the Spirit aims at unity. The first public proclamation of the Gospel was to overcome ethnic divisions and unite the world. We have our own divisions, splits, differences hitherto irreconcilable. They exist in families, factories, social gatherings, cities. Political and diplomatic maneuverings can't patch them up. The world, like Humpty Dumpty, has had a great fall, splitting it apart. All the king's horses and all the king's men can't put it together again.

The deeper unity so desirable is a spiritual gift. The spiritual gifts enumerated in 1 Corinthians 12 all help to make us one in and with Christ. This larger, deeper, and closer global unity the world knows nothing of and finds unachievable.

The French phrase, *esprit de corps*, defined as "a sense of union and of common interests and responsibilities, as developed among a group of persons associated together," is translatable into our "teamwork." The Spirit engages all who belong to the body of Christ to live and work together as a team. He has the same unifying role among us as in the Trinity. In the Trinity the Father and the Son are one, and so Christ commissions his Spirit to make mankind "one like us" (Jn 17:11).

4. Degrees of unity

Various degrees of unity are possible to man, ranging all the way from a casual meeting in the smoker, at a bar or cocktail party, to the mystical union of God and his saints. The union brought about by the Spirit is closer than any we know in our closest human relationships. We attribute this fact to the "real kinship between the human spirit and the divine" (H. Wheeler Robinson, *The Christian Experience of the Holy Spirit*, p. 242). The experience of this kinship is heady; it leaves man "floating on air." "He is conscious of living 'in' God in a way far deeper than he can be said to live in the life of his friends or they to live in him. His own personality has been integrated into a larger personality" (ibid., p. 234).

What cripples, stunts, dwarfs the effect of unity among us is the media the Spirit has to use. He seeks to express unity in media subordinate to himself. We Christians snub his effectiveness by the petty, selfish, conflicting use of his gifts, his aids to promote the ministry and service of the Church to the world. Christians can give no better service and witness than a unified spirit to a world disintegrating and groaning for unity.

Solemnity of the Most Holy Trinity
Dt 4:32-34, 39-40; Rm 8:14-17; Mt 28:16-20

Homesick for Heaven

1. Our need of home

"Our most deeply felt need is our need of home," remarked a biblical commentator on Romans 8:12-17. We
may have needs more necessary for survival but none *so
deeply felt* as our need for home. I recall my own experience away from home for the first time, my first year in
the seminary. I became homesick and one lonely night
cried myself to sleep. It was tempting to leave the seminary and return to the love, comfort, and familiarity of
home.

Life is tinged with a sense of homesickness. The reason
is that God our Creator and Father makes his home in
heaven, and being his issue, we belong to him. "Yahweh
is God indeed, in heaven above and on earth beneath."
Our homesickness for heaven doesn't spring from pre-
existence, from once having been in heaven, as if we were
born there and awaken to life upon earth. Our homesickness is typified in St. Augustine's prayer to the Lord, "You
have made us for yourself, and our heart is restless until
it rests in you" (*Confessions*, Bk. 1, Chapt. 1).

2. Baptized into sons of God

Baptism sets us on a new way of life, the way to heav-
en. Each of us realizes the execution of Christ's command,
"Baptize them in the name of the Father and the Son and
of the Hody Spirit." The Spirit transformed us into sons
of God. He conferred on us a sonship similar to that which

Jesus had in Mary's womb. The reality of sonship began then, but its realization grows upon us. The "spirit of sons" stirs in us a longing for our heirdom. As long as we're "heirs of God and coheirs with Christ" we're not going to feel fully content until we've arrived in our heavenly home. The baptismal grace or spirit leaves us somewhat homesick.

The sacrament of baptism and its benefits marks us off from all others. It's a priceless and extraordinary gift which symbolizes God's search for us. He sought us out to adopt us as sons who were only one variety of his myriad creations. Thinking of the millions of people who are still non-Christian, the idea of our adoption comes to mind. Study the history of religions and see how many ethnic groups sought out a god to worship. Necessity was the mother of their inventions. They discovered gods for their homes, fields, wars, peace, etc. Their gods loved, married, propagated; they acted too humanly.

Their religious experience is opposite to ours. They sought God, he found and chose us. Their gods numbered many, ours is only one. Israel is the story of a people God chose for his very own. "They were adopted as sons," says St. Paul (Rm 9:4), to keep alive the belief and worship of the one true God. The central theme of the Christian gospel, which follows in the wake of Israel's story and is a much richer theme, states how God acted in Christ and chose us to become his children, his heirs.

3. Effects of adoption

Our adoption into God's family is a deep mystery, truly the deepest mystery of our faith. Christ introduced us to this mystery while introducing himself. The awareness and knowledge of the two mysteries, Christ and the Trinity, developed historically hand in hand. The two mysteries overlap and also shed light upon each other. If you like a mystery—most people do—you'll find the Trinity most fascinating. The more searchingly you look for your adoptive God, the more intimately you call him "Father," the more trustingly you depend on him, the more lovingly you live for him, the closer you're taken into his trinitarian life. The fascination with the Trinity never ends.

Our adoption is more understandable in the cultural context of the Near East. According to Roman Law, adoption meant coming under the authority of a new father, but in the Near East it meant principally becoming his heir. Our admission into God's family is a gift of sheer love. By reason of this gift we become heirs of heaven, sharers with Christ of our own true home. We feel the realism of this gift in our sense of longing to be with God.

We're not entirely at home with others until we've all been taken into his heavenly household. We're not completely at ease till we come into his home environment. Observe how all men seek happiness. Life upon earth can be full of happy moments, yet none lasts long enough to rejoice men always. They're merely diversions or distractions compared to divine enjoyment. We shall be freer, healthier, infinitely more satisfied in God's company. He will have saved us, each of us, in a common life.

4. Related to the Trinity

God isn't a loner, living in a lonely and isolated way. His life consists of a living and loving exchange within a Trinity of Persons. The Father-Son-Spirit relationship we point to with the exterior sign of baptism, and with our countless signs of the cross. But in reality theirs is a relationship we can never fathom.

The triune relationship which makes God happy he extends to us, even now. We speak of this in Christian tradition as the indwelling of the Trinity. The Father and Son and Holy Spirit dwell in us in return for our love of Christ: "we shall come to him (one who loves Christ) and make our home with him" (Jn 14:23).

Human life is interpersonal. We're persons-in-relation to others, especially to those we hold dear in our family home. Life with God adds a further dimension to all social life, even to that of a family. Away from our family home for a while, and away from our true home with God, we may feel homesick.

Solemnity of Corpus Christi
Ex 24:3-8; Heb 9:11-15; Mk 14:12-16, 22-26

Lifeblood

Did you ever donate blood? How many of you have—
may we have a show of hands? Some of you may have accepted blood donations. Either experience affords a good
insight into the ancient Hebrew esteem for blood. In their
mind, blood was equivalent to the spirit of life; it gave
vital strength. They identified it with life. Too much loss
of blood meant dying. Could the ancient Hebrews see
us today, they would marvel at the human ability to store
up blood in banks and ship it overseas.

1. The blood of the covenant

The Hebrew practice of using blood in sacrificial worship, though it looked like a bloody mess, made consider-
able sense. Moses, who wasn't a priest (at that time anybody could offer worship), inaugurated this practice in
memory of God's liberation of Israel from Egypt and the
covenant on Mt. Sinai. He made it mandatory in the form
of a peace offering to God. The ritual custom was to take
animal blood—of calves, bulls, goats—and sprinkle half on
the altar representative of God and half on the people.
Blood symbolized the covenant (bond or link) God had
with Israel. The covenant was written (that is, ratified or
sealed) in blood, symbolizing the vital relationship between God and his people. Without that blood flowing
between the altar and the worshippers, they were no longer vitally associated with him; they were a dead people.

The blood transfused from donor to recipient must be
of the same type. The blood is typed first, then volun-

teered. The blood Jesus offered at the Last Supper and later sacrificed on the cross was the same human type as ours. His lifeblood was transfused into us at those two events according to the ancient Hebrew belief that "it is blood that atones for a life" (Lv 17:11). The original covenant was a transfusion of life between God and his people. The new covenant ratified or sealed in Jesus' blood gives us a share in the life of God. The latter covenant is far superior to the former because the blood Jesus spilled for love of us was his own.

2. A gift

You know as well as I that a pint of blood can save a life. It may make all the difference between life and death. This difference suggests the near-infinite value attached to life. Sometimes we resort to extraordinary means to preserve it. Their esteem for life prompts many people to donate blood without asking for payment. They regard life as a gift, something we neither lay claim to nor cling to.

Jesus was, in a spiritual sense, the *first* blood donor, and his gift was life forever. "This is my blood," he offered at the Last Supper, "the blood of the covenant, which is to be poured out for many." His cross was the first red cross, the saving remedy for the sins of mankind. His sacrificial act continues under the symbol of wine. If life itself has incalculable value, surely the life coming from the bloody death upon the cross has a value beyond our comprehension. "How much more effectively the blood of Christ, who offered himself as the perfect sacrifice to God through the eternal Spirit, can purify our inner self from dead actions so that we do our service to the living God."

3. The transfusion of life

Life is a mystery, but life with Christ is more mysterious yet. The transfusion of his life into ours takes place mysteriously, spiritually, under the symbol of wine. The stronger our belief in this sacramental symbol, the more effective the transfusion of his life into ours. A pint of his lifeblood can save us for eternity. "I tell you most solemnly, if you do not eat the flesh of the Son of Man and drink his blood, you will not have life in you. Anyone who does eat my flesh and drink my blood has eternal life, and I shall raise him up on the last day" (Jn 6:53-54).

That Christ calls his a blood *of the covenant* means more than my having a blood affinity with him. I have such with my in-laws. He gives me a lifeblood relationship with him, linking us lovingly together. I must respond to this gift. "Because you have saved my life, cured it, healed it of sin, I intend always to love you, Jesus, and to be at your service. I can only exchange my life with yours. The life I expend in the service of my fellowmen is a homage paid to you. Your lifeblood has brought me in closer ties with my fellowmen than I otherwise would have been capable of. With your lifeblood coursing through my veins, you stand at the center of every human relationship. I can never be grateful enough for the gift of your lifeblood."

4. Spiritual anemia

The lack of sufficient healthy blood is called "anemia." Blood transfusions are particularly helpful for the anemic. Christians can contract a sickness we may call "spiritual anemia." In the practice of their faith they are pale, weak, they have little or no get up and go. An examination of their lives would prove that they deprive themselves of the spiritual food and drink of the Eucharist. Or the cause for their anemic condition may well be their half-hearted, routine reception of the Eucharistic Christ, which is the more pitiable because his blood is so rich in divine life.

5. New wine, new life

The Christian life is so interfused with Christ that it

doesn't stop with physical death. This is in part the meaning of his parting remark in the supper hall: "I tell you solemnly, I shall not drink any more wine until the day I drink the new wine in the kingdom of God." "But now Christ has come, as the high priest of all the blessings which were to come." The present Christian life leads us directly into the blessed future life with Christ. The Eucharistic Christ offers us the hope of everlasting life, the lease upon a new life. That life will be new and complete, unfailing and indescribable.

SEASON OF THE YEAR

Tenth Sunday of the Year
Gn 3:9-15; 2 Cor 4:14-5:1; Mk 3:20-35

The Secret Agent

1. A world invisible

At the end of this homily, we will all stand up to make our profession of faith, saying that we believe in the maker "of all that is seen and unseen." The world we see, we know exists because we see it. We see the heavens and the earth, the sun, moon, stars, the plant and animal life, the beautiful flowers decorating our lawns, the vegetables served at table, the meats. The world of the senses really exists because it offers tangible proof of itself. But there is an invisible world that really exists too, and in this we're asked to believe. "Only faith can . . . prove the existence of the realities that at present remain unseen" (Heb 11:1).

The Scriptures attest to it time and again, that there is a world far larger, closer to us, and more wonderful than the world we see. Another world is present to us and influential, of which we're not so conscious as we are of the visible world. The invisible world is here and now.

During the winter season, when the earth lies dull and barren, it looks as if no life were hidden in it, and yet we know that its power is asleep, hidden. The animal world too instills in us a sense of mystery. The animal instinct is able to communicate among animals in a way beyond our understanding. If even the visible world confronts us with mystery, why should we refuse to believe in an unseen world?

2. Evil spirits

The Scriptures attempt to describe a world of spirits as well as a world of the senses. Among the spirits existing in the other world God holds the first rank, and he has under him a hierarchy of angels and saints. The spirits of the dead continue to exist there but cease to appeal to us through our senses. Apart from God, Christ, the angels and saints, but in the same unseen world, there exists a company of evil spirits. They make up the number of the Enemy, and go by the name of Satan or Devil and their companions.

Devilish forces or demonic powers are sometimes said not to exist, that they're the product of the imagination. We have no certain evidence of their existence. The evil we see in this world, we're inclined to attribute to some outside evil force. People who hold such an opinion make one wonder if the amount and intensity of evil in this world are of human making alone?

The opposite tendency among some believers is to exaggerate the influence of evil spirits in this world. They see Satan at work everywhere. They magnify his power into that of a god. However difficult it may be to differentiate humanly instigated evil from the devilish, they're ready to give Satan too much credit.

3. The evidence for satan

What position does the Church take in regard to these two tendencies, the one verging upon denial of Satan, the other upon superstition? Its long-standing practice, based upon the Bible, has been to teach the existence of a world of spirits, both good and evil. This invisible world has a bearing upon our life, to make or break us. Because the evidence for it, biblical or otherwise, isn't as foolproof as for the visible world, room is left for doubt at least in some instances where, say, evil results are ascribed too easily to the work of the Devil.

This was the case in the life and work of Jesus himself. His own relatives thought him insane if not possessed by the Devil. His enemies charged him with working wonders by the power of Satan, one of whose names in the Bible is Beelzebul, the lord of flies, the prince of devils, the same who tempted Eve. In the Genesis story, however, Eve blames her fall into sin upon an evil spirit who takes the form of a serpent: "The serpent tempted me and I ate." Jesus' counter-argument to the religious leaders was that if his power came from Satan, then Satan wouldn't destroy his own kingdom or rule. In other words, neither then nor now is Satan in any way about to work against himself or ruin his own efforts.

Satan is much too smart and sly to expose himself openly, to let us know beyond the shadow of a doubt about his existence and especially about his influence. If he were too familiar with us, we just might resist him bore strenuously. Can you imagine how attractive he would be to people if he were to frighten them out of their wits? Picture him as ugly as you can, and you will have people disbelieving in him or keeping their distance from him. St. Paul was more realistic about him in trying to impress the Corinthians "with his cunning" (2 Cor 11:3).

4. Accuser and enemy

The Satan pictured in the Bible has two roles. The one is of an accuser, the other of an adversary or enemy. He appears in both roles in the book of Job. Satan and his fellow spirits are master spies forever around and prying into our lives, digging up every bit of dirt against us, sifting out whatever evidence of evil they can. The major attempt of any and every devilish spirit is to make evil predominate over good. Bad news has to prevail in a world which God found to be good and where Christ brought the Good News of salvation.

Satan is a master spy, but more so a secret agent who tempted the first man and woman and continues to tempt every man. Man is no match for his superhuman power. This fact is confirmed by those who had dealings with him. They will tell you in so many stories of his power, mysterious and unpredictable.

To fool around with Satan is to get ourselves caught in a kingdom divided, a house divided. We can't flirt with Satan and at the same time expect to belong to a new world to come where with Christ we will wake up to eternal peace and enjoyment.

Eleventh Sunday of the Year
Ez 17:22-24; 2 Cor 5:6-10; Mk 4:26-34

The Coming Kingdom

1. From shrub to kingdom

It may sound slangy or informal, but what Jesus means by "birds" in his story of them nesting and nestling in the mustard bush is *people*, the nations of the world, especially the Gentile nations. In other words, the kingdom of God will be filled with you "birds," implying that birds of a feather—those who believe in him and his kingdom—will flock together there at the end of time. By gathering the Gentile peoples into his kingdom, Jesus lets us see his kingdom already in the process of realization.

He compares the kingdom of God not so much to a tiny seed as to a tall shrub, to a final stage of growth. The tall shrub, full-grown, stands about eight to ten feet high and attracts the birds with its shade for shelter and seed for food. The tall bush that provides shelter and food is already in the Old Testament (Ezk 17:23) a figure of speech for a mighty kingdom which protects its peoples.

In addition to the comparison there's the contrast between the kingdom at its beginning and at its end. How can something so little grow into something so large? Out of the littlest, most insignificant, and invisible things God builds his mighty and world-wide kingdom.

2. No dreamland

The kingdom of God, whatever we may think of it,

isn't a dream world. Every once in a while some work of the imagination appears in print to picture a future world which tickles our fancy. The *Utopia* of Thomas More, written in 1516, was a work of this kind. Its very title explains that Utopia is *not a place*. It describes an imaginary island where the peoples enjoy the utmost perfection in social, economic, political, and cultural life. The kingdom of God, on the contrary, is invisible to the human eye but real.

The world Jesus has in mind and preaches is a kingdom of *God*, not a *man*-made world. It definitely isn't a kingdom of success, of money, of earthly possessions, of political or economic power, of pleasure, or popularity or social standing. All such thoughts of and plans for the world are bound to fail, ultimately, for they don't reckon with the kingdom of God.

3. Recasting the world

Prophetic-minded men, like Thomas More in his story of *Utopia* and Jacques Maritain in *Integral Humanism*, are warning us against a misconception of this world, its present and future. We ought to listen to them, men who have the wisdom to know and judge the ways of the world.

Four centuries after Thomas More, Jacques Maritain evaluates the world as follows: "Modern civilization is a wornout garment. One cannot sew new pieces on it. It requires a total and, I may say, substantial recasting, a transvaluation of cultural principles: since it is a question of arriving at a vital primacy of quality over quantity, of work over money, of the human over the technological, of wisdom over science, of the common service of human persons over the individual covetousness of unlimited enrichment or the State's covetousness of unlimited power" (p. 207).

And who will be able to recast human civilization?

Who will be able to transvaluate or change its principles for the better? Not man alone surely, for he brought it to this sorry state. The Maritain statement confirms what Jesus was saying: "Mine is not a kingdom of this world" (Jn 18:36). The kingdom of God will come about only through the act of divine power. God alone can realize it, he alone has absolute power over life, growth, death. He stunts and gives growth, he withers and makes the meadows green again.

4. The kingdom already

The prospect of his kingdom begins with the announcement: "The time has come," he said, "and the kingdom of God is close at hand. Repent, and believe the Good News" (Mk 1:15). The Good News is broadcast to all men, the theme of his preaching. For those who welcome it and receive it wholeheartedly, the kingdom of God is already a saving event in their lives.

The details—the when and the where—of the growth or spread of the kingdom of God are left out of Jesus' message or remain unclear. We only know that he will come again to rule and judge the world. He himself will set the final stage of the kingdom—"how, he does not know." "Each of us will (then) get what he deserves for the things he did in the body, good or bad."

5. Be patient and confident

The story of the mustard seed and shrub reassures those who look over the world situation today, find it pitiful, and with heavy hearts wonder whether the kingdom of God will ever come. This world-view is not much different from the experience of some disciples of Jesus in his time. They too had doubts about his kingdom. Will the almighty power of God ever win out against the evils of the world?

Remember, Jesus didn't come to change the kingdom or empires of this world, nor to organize any economic and political revolution of human society. He didn't promise a heaven upon earth.

The story of the tall shrub affording shelter and food for the "birds," and the present state of world affairs, sound a call to patience and humble confidence. "Now be patient, brothers, until the Lord's coming . . . (which) will be soon" (Jm 5:7f.). While we are patient night and day, awake and asleep, time is passing into the eternal kingdom of God where there will be mercy, joy, peace, and achievement.

If life in the world has been hard for you, if you have suffered much, if you have found it to be a test for your faith, if you have been wondering if God will let this world go to pot, I assure you that you can look forward to his kingdom to come "full of confidence."

Twelfth Sunday of the Year
Jb 38:1, 8-11; 2 Cor 5:14-17; Mk 4:35-41

Do You Not Care?

1. A miracle-story

About a third of the gospel by Mark is taken up with miracle-stories, the wonders God worked in the life of Jesus. Mark adds journalistic details not to be found in the other gospels. He mentions, for example, that Jesus was asleep with a cushion under his head. He relates too the question the disciples put to him after awaking him, "Master, do you not care?"

The setting of this miracle-story is the Lake of Galilee, a fairly large and beautiful lake surrounded with cliffs, where the followers of Christ, fishermen, do their fishing. Many a time Jesus preaches from a boat on this lake to the crowds that line its shores.

But this Galilean lake is also known for its sudden storms. The plot of the miracle-story is that Jesus and his disciples are caught in such a storm, while he remains asleep and they're afraid of capsizing and drowning.

2. Harking back to creation

Besides imagining the natural setting of this incident, we need to back it up with Old Testament stories of creation and the flood in order to understand it fully. In the beginning of time and space, the land and sea compose a chaos. The sea is like a sea dragon or demon, terrible and chaotic. With the power of his word, God divides the land from the sea and sets them in order, calms the sea. The fact that he has power over the elements shows that he is God. "With his power he calmed the Sea (Jb 26:12). "You control the pride of the ocean, when its waves ride high you calm them" (Ps 89:9).

Jesus has only to *speak* to the storm-tossed sea, and it calms down. The word he uses to still the sea is the same in Mark as in the Greek text of Genesis 8:1. His word and effect make the disciples wonder: "Who can this be? Even the wind and the sea obey him." He astonishes his disciples by accomplishing what only God can do.

3. The ark and the boat

We gain a further insight into the miracle-story by recalling that in Christian tradition the fishing boat stands for the Church. Jesus' first disciples were fishermen by trade but became fishers of men in the Church. The symbol of the fishing boat goes back in association to Noah's Ark, which, with Noah's family, God rescued from the flood. We ought to see here a transition from the idea of creation to that of redemption. The two realities go together. God abandons neither his creation nor redemption in his Church.

The marvel Jesus performs on the Lake of Galilee is a sign of a new age. He begins the new creation. "The new creation has begun to exist in it (the Church)" (Romano Guardini, *The Life of Faith*, p. 107).

4. In the same boat

The miracle-story has much more meaning for us in the Church today if we put ourselves imaginatively in that storm-tossed boat and think over the questions Jesus and his disciples put to each other. Upon awakening him, they ask, "Master, do you not care?" Their question sounds as if they're charging him with neglect, disinterest, unconcern.

But it would be unfair of us to see them so frightened for their own selves without seeing ourselves in the same

boat, in the present-day Church. To some Christians the
situation looks as if Christ were sleeping within the
Church while it is sinking, sucking us all along with it.
They expect the Church to ride through unruffled waters
of life and arrive safely, without disturbing them too much,
at the shores of heaven. They don't seem to realize the
need for faith in the Church in the midst of storm and
stress. They're asking Christ, "Don't you care about us?"

Others have the notion that the Church isn't ploughing
through the sea at all but resting in dry dock, hoisted out
of the tide of human events. They doubt whether the
Church today is the great sign of salvation to all men. It
appears leaky, creaky, and split as any human institution.
It's altogether too human. Yet despite all its frailty, from
the boat of the Church we hear the word of God and feel
its power still at work. Nobody is to blame for leaving the
boat if and when it tries to sail on human power alone.
But ours is the Church of *Christ,* and in him we need to
believe.

5. Of little faith

When the windstorm hit the Lake of Galilee suddenly,
the disciples didn't call out to Christ for help while he was
walking the water or standing ashore. He was in the boat
as really as he's in the Church today. His reply to them
is unmistakably a judgment. "Why are you so frightened?
How is it that you have no faith?" Mark doesn't soften the
blow of his words. "How is it that you have *no* faith?"
You can find the same saying in Matthew and Luke, but
apologetically they take the zing out of it: ". . . you men
of little faith," "Where is your faith?" (Mt 8:26; Lk 8:25).
We should consider the real words of Christ addressed to
ourselves in the Church today.

By a terrible twist of fate, the same disciples who fear
that Christ will sleep through their crisis, who feel he has
no care for them, later in life fall asleep on him. The scene

is Gethsemane, and this time, in his distress, a sudden fear comes upon Christ himself. Sorrowful to the point of death, he asks his disciples, "Wait here, and keep awake" (Mk 14:34). He goes aside to pray for a while, then returns to find them sleeping. "You should be awake," he says to Peter, "and praying not to be put to the test" (Mk 14:37).

Whenever our Church is in a crisis, whenever its members are in danger of being swamped by some storm, we needn't worry that it will tip over like a boat. Christ is in the boat. He may appear to be sleeping, but he has the power of God to save us. We should rather examine ourselves. Have we been asleep when we should have been praying, giving aid to Christ in the needs of the Church?

Thirteenth Sunday of the Year
Ws 1:13-15, 2:23-24; 2 Cor 8:7, 9, 13-15; Mk 5:21-43

Wonderful Are Your Works

1. Questions of life and death

The series of statements in the first reading, excerpted from the book of Wisdom, one of the Old Testament books full of wise sayings from the ancient past, seem contradictory to the two cases described in the gospel of Mark. "Death is not God's doing . . . God did make man imperishable . . . the world's created things have health in them." If God makes man imperishable, why did he let Jairus' daughter die? If created things have health in them, why was the woman hemorrhaging twelve years? Or why should any one of us have to suffer and die? Is the Bible caught in a contradiction? Does God go back upon his word?

The Bible certainly tackles the questions of life and death, but it would be hard to prove from biblical data alone that man was originally destined to live forever upon earth, or to be free from accident, sickness, and disease. Whether man started life out in an earthly paradise is a moot question. But one thing the Bible makes clear and sure: the destiny of man isn't death but life, and life forever. Death, in the biblical sense, isn't merely a bodily or physical dying. Nor is it only sin but the useless existence of the sinner. Anyone who thinks the life of man is only this-worldly has a mistaken philosophy of life. No greater lie exists than to live life without the thought of survival after death.

Neither Jairus, the Jewish synagogue official, nor the woman with the hemorrhage threw the life/death question up to God. Their concern was a restoration to life and to health. The double miracle illustrates how men and women at that time accepted miracles.

2. Wonder and belief

Are we less inclined to accept miracles and more prone to question God and his providence? We ask ourselves why an all-good and all-loving and all-powerful God should permit so much evil and misery in human life. We puzzle over *why* God acts one way, the ancients wondered *how* they could get God to act in another way. They set a pattern of thinking and believing that we might well emulate. They found God wonderful in his works.

The double miracle-story hinges upon the pre-condition of faith to the working of wonders. To Jairus Jesus says, "Do not be afraid; only have faith." And to the frightened but healed woman who admitted the truth to him, he replied, "Your faith has restored you to health." So neither of the two miracles happens automatically or magically; they depend upon faith. Other persons in the crowd jostling around Jesus and pushing against him may not have been in good health or had someone dying back home. Jesus doesn't help them, because they don't seek his help. God won't save us despite ourselves; he expects us to be convinced of his power, goodness, and mercy, and to trust in him. Two elements in the faith of Jairus and the woman are conviction and trust.

3. The right approach

The woman who elbowed her way through the crowd behind Jesus to touch his clothes had exhausted all human help and was becoming worse rather than better. Taking the last human resort, she acted in close cooperation with Jesus—*she touched him.* People who keep their distance from God or Jesus, who hardly lift a finger in their own behalf, who let others run all their errands for them, who think of divine providence as some sort of welfare system, won't receive the divine help. God helps those who help themselves. We must do better than stand at the edge of a crowd, we must approach Jesus with outstretched hands, we must touch him.

Jairus too feels the need for active cooperation with Jesus, so he invites him to his home to lay hands on his daughter. His part in the double miracle-story differs from the other: he expressly *asks* for help. How is Jesus humanly to know that Jairus wants his daughter healed and saved if he doesn't ask. The extraordinary things in life God is unlikely to do for us without the asking. He may know our needs before we ask him, but we whet our appetites for his gifts by the asking. He'll give us of his surplus when we show our need.

I can't promise you that God will perform marvels in your favor if you pre-condition yourself in the way Jairus and the woman did, but I can assure you that they had the right approach. With faith in Jesus, they actively cooperated with him, and begged him to use his power, goodness, and mercy for their sake. Jesus appreciates this approach: "I tell you therefore: everything you ask and pray for, believe that you have it already, and it will be yours" (Mk 11:24).

4. Building the kingdom

Though every miracle, every restoration to health and to life looks forward to the greatest miracle of all, the resurrection from sin and Satan to a new life, miracles help to build up the kingdom of God already. "In Christ's word, in His works, and in His presence this kingdom reveals itself to men . . . The miracles of Jesus also confirm that the kingdom has already arrived on earth" (*Constitution on the Church,* #5). People with no faith in miracles, who may even laugh at the idea as they laughed at Jesus when he came to Jairus' home to raise his daughter to life, can't belong to the kingdom of God. They lack the pre-condition to life in such a kingdom.

The connection between faith, miracle, and kingdom is very close. All of them together compose the wonderful works of God. A miracle is a sign of faith on the one hand, and a sign of God's kingdom on the other. It stands between faith and the kingdom, and eventually faith and miracle will pass into the eternal kingdom of God, where we'll meet and live with the Wonder of all wonders.

Fourteenth Sunday of the Year
Ezk 2:2-5; 2 Cor 12:7-10; Mk 6:1-6

Prophet Without Honor

This little letter, printed in the original handwriting, appeared in "Letters to the Editor," a daily newspaper column:

"Gentlemen:

My teacher wants us to bring in happy news. I looked through the paper and couldn't find any. So I am asking you if you could put more happy news in the paper.

Yours truly,
Beth Geary."

1. No good news

Two thoughts came to mind when I read this and clipped it out. The first was that this grade school child was so right. The child speaking its mind, was telling the truth about ourselves. Christ blessed God "for hiding these things from the learned and the clever and revealing them to mere children" (Mt 11:25).

My afterthought was that no happy news would come from this request. The newspapers would heed neither this child nor the Scripture: "Guard against foul talk; let your words be for the improvement of others, as occasion offers, and do good to your listeners (or readers). . ." (Ep 4:29). Happy news may be scarce for want of happy events, but what else is fit to print?

2. Reaction to Jesus

This story updates the experience Jesus had in his

hometown. The hometownspeople gave him no gala reception. They heard him speak in their synagogue, and "most of them were astonished" at his wisdom and power. Even with a local newspaper, they would have run no such headline, "Hometown Boy Makes Good." Their reaction to him was typical of those who weren't prepared for the Good News. "And they would not accept him," because they lacked faith in him. And perhaps too, out of envy born of familiarity with him and his parents, they were tempted to cut him down to their own size. Their first enthusiasm wore off, doubt set in, then opposition, and at last they rejected him.

Jesus was about as amazed at their lack of faith as they were at his wisdom and power. "A prophet," he said, "is only despised in his own country, among his own relations and in his own house."

3. In/out of season

Whether or not the preaching of the Good News is effective, isn't the bugging question. It *is* effective, undoubtedly. The real question is whether or not to preach it in case no good results will accrue from it. When to keep silent, when to speak out? Living in a post-Christian world, do we Christians have any social responsibility to make our views known, or should we confine our concern and attention merely to individuals who voluntarily give us a hearing? The answer lies in the life of the prophet Ezekiel.

He had, most probably, both rebels and exiles to address. A man convinced of God's presence in the world and his hand in world events, he felt compelled to disclose the "wholly other" side of life. First he had to "stand up" and listen to God's message and its meaning, however harsh they were. "Whether they listen or not," God then contended, "This set of rebels shall know there is a prophet among them." People may be able to ignore God's messengers but not God.

In our day, the outspoken are ostracized from their country and certain topics of conversation and public concern are considered taboo. The unmentionables—are we to clamp up about them or sweep them under the rug of oblivion? Specific issues, almost too sticky to handle— divorce, abortion, contraception, overpopulation, injustice, dishonesty, poverty, mercy-killing, sterilization?

4. Apply the gospel

The objection repeated against the Church's voice in social problems is that she can't know all the facts in this highly complex society. Some problems are so acute they need immediate, short-term, and expedient solutions. Society can't wait for the more patient and long-range solutions the Church offers. She reasons too abstractly, she isn't versed enough in empirical knowledge. Well, should she avoid this criticism by letting matters be? No, she has skilled and knowledgeable laypeople to speak for her and for Christ. "Even though Christians may at times err in their facts, interpretations, and conclusions about social issues, they must not fail to apply the Gospel to contemporary life" (*To Teach As Jesus Did, A Pastoral Message on Christian Education,* #61).

The Church today admits she doesn't have pat solutions to all modern-day problems. She's willing, in reply to critics who tell her to mind her own business, to confess her weaknesses. Church-goers must take an example from St. Paul, a man pestered by a chronic ailment, who had to live with it, "quite content with (his) weaknesses." His weakness didn't prevent the Lord from exerting his power at its best in him.

5. Society versus the Church

The weakness isn't all on the side of the Church which speaks out. It may be on the side of her listeners too, or of those who fail to listen. Are society's leaders open to solutions other than their own? What dispositions, what attitudes do *they* have toward the Church? Do they stop up their ears or hear only what they want to hear? A society almost totally secular leaves itself open to the anti-God perversions of man and the world—to self-seeking, power, and delusion.

The Gospel lesson is Christ without honor among his own people, through no fault of his own.

Fifteenth Sunday of the Year
Am 7:12-15; Ep 1:3-14; Mk 6:7-13

A Church of Poverty

1. Prophecy and poverty

The Church and the prophet Amos are accused of the same fault—commercialization. Amos was faulted by the priest Amaziah for professionalizing and commercializing prophecy. In other words, for being interested only in fees. He was ordered out of the country (the Northern Kingdom of Israel). The same accusation befalls any one or any group that runs religion for a profit.

Truthfully, Amos was no professional prophet. He prophesied in obedience to the Lord: "Go, prophecy to my people Israel." He was a shepherd by trade and moon-lighted as a dresser of sycamores because he was poor. The fruit of the sycamore was the food of the poor.

Neglect of keeping poverty and of attending to the poor is one of the most serious criticisms brought against the Church. Poverty is a necessary quality of the Church in every age, just as necessary as unity or apostolicity or catholicity or holiness, although these four are named the marks of the Church. She's recognizable by her marks.

2. The poor Christ

The Church must be poor in imitation of her Master. Jesus gave up his occupation as a carpenter in order to fend for himself in his public life. He called no place his home: "Foxes have holes and the birds of the air have nests, but the Son of Man has nowhere to lay his head" (Mt 8:20). He pledged himself to a life of poverty: "he was rich, but he became poor for your sake, to make you rich out of his poverty" (2 Cor 8:9). In the possession and distribution of grace he was infinitely rich. On the other hand, he emptied himself of personal and material possessions, assuming the condition of a servant (Ph 2:7).

This pattern of poverty was taken over by his disciples, upon his advice. He advised them about poverty at an opportune moment, immediately before they went into his service. The key idea he proposed then was *detachment* from food, clothing, home, possessions. Notice how he joined service with poverty, as if to say: Travel lightly, for the more burdened you are, the less service you can render.

3. The poor Church

The history of the Church evidences the fact that she prospered in poverty. The first converts were poor Galilean fishermen. And most early converts came from the poor. At first they had no buildings of their own to gather in. They worshipped in the synagogues as long as they could. Then they took to their private homes for worship. Whenever the Church became rich, especially after Constantine in 312 gave her political peace and endowed her, she drove people away from herself. She was criticized and persecuted then. Her wealth seemed like a threat of impoverishment for others. The same predicament besets the Church as often as she enriches herself with money, buildings, and lands.

At a moment in her history when people seemed to be kind to her, when she seemed to be riding the crest of peace and popularity, Pope John XXIII reminded the Church of her holy obligation to be a "Church of the poor." Pope John was like a householder who lived a long time in his old home place. Without realizing it, the Church accumulated much "junk" in the past. Pope John wanted to make a clean sweep of it, "to shake off the dust of the

Empire that has gathered since Constantine's day on the throne of St. Peter."

Material wealth tempts the Church with a sense of security. A moneyed and propertied Church is left not with the "look of poverty" but with the "appearance of riches." Christ drove the money-changers out of the temple once; he does so again and again.

4. Genuinely rich

The Church is truly rich, really blessed when gifted with the Spirit of Christ. Look over St. Paul's list of blessings. Sons of God, remitted of our sins, sealed by the Holy Spirit—what more can we ask for in the Church? We have already the first installment of our future inheritance.

Poverty means coming down a notch or two, having nothing to brag about. Since the real absolute values of life aren't superficial or of passing fancy, poverty means getting rid of Church buildings and furnishings, ornaments, vessels, vestments, and marks of honor that belong to another age. If poverty is a mark of the Church, a mark of poverty is simplicity. ". . . less *of* the world and more *for* the world" (Yves Congar, *Power and Poverty in the Church,* p. 141).

Having abandoned the accumulations of her past, the Church is free and open to the future. "What the past has made us is yet to come" (Johannes Baptist Metz, *Poverty of Spirit,* p. 40f.). The Church is poor and incomplete because of her pioneering and pacesetting spirit, not having arrived yet in the promised land.

5. Poor and serviceable

Christians who in a spirit of justice and charity concern themselves with the socioeconomic development of the world will be permeated with a spirit of poverty (cf. *Constitution on the Church in the Modern World,* #72).

Priests and bishops are to devote whatever benefits remain from their decent livelihood and fulfillment of duties to the good of the Church or to works of charity (cf. *Decree on the Ministry and Life of Priests,* #17).

Religious are to "avoid every appearance of luxury, of excessive wealth, and accumulation of possessions" (*Decree on the Appropriate Renewal of the Religious Life,* #13).

The call and mission of the Church to be poor and serviceable is urgent. Don't pack away too much, travel lightly, for the way of life is short and the time brief.

Sixteenth Sunday of the Year
Jr 23:1-6; Ep 2:13-18; Mk 6:30-34

The Truth About Man

A character, Julia by name, in Evelyn Waugh's once
best-selling novel, *Brideshead Revisited,* speaks of her husband Rex as follows:

"You know Father Mowbray hit on the truth about
Rex at once, that it took me a year of marriage to see.
He simply wasn't all there. He wasn't a complete human being at all. He was a tiny bit of one, unnaturally
developed: something in a bottle, an organ kept alive
in a laboratory. I thought he was a sort of primitive
savage, but he was something absolutely modern and
up-to-date that only this ghastly age could produce. A
tiny bit of a man pretending he was the whole."

1. Man below and above par

Sad to say, this description of Julia's husband fits the
secularistic and material-minded man of today. Man without Christ for his ideal and image is the diminished man,
the dwarfed human. Much of modern human life can
hardly be called human; indeed it has become sub-human.
Not even animals treat one another as we sometimes do.
And much if not all this mistreatment springs from a neglect of the Pauline teaching that Christ became man "to
create one single New Man in himself." The basis of the
new humanity is Christ. Christ unites all mankind in himself; for he's "the peace between us," "destroying in his
own person the hostility" between Jew and Gentile, and
among all peoples.

"Ah, what is man. . .?" asks the Psalmist (8:4). And the answer is: only God really knows, and he reveals man fully in the life of his Son Jesus. Whoever refuses to learn from him what human life is all about, will be less the man. Only in Christ can each of us put on "the new self that has been created in God's way, in the goodness and holiness of the truth" (Ep 4:24).

2. Man self-enclosed and goalless

Man remains a mystery to himself as long as he doesn't direct his life to a goal beyond himself or beyond nature. Man whose life is self-enclosed is like a turtle pulling his neck within his shell. He must come out of himself, transcend himself.

Man without a single goal in life is like a shattered mirror which reflects no single image. His real image is superimposed on him by Christ. The Christian view of man is copied from that image—Christ, projected to us by a Person—Christ. Christians looking upon Christ behold in him the true man. They don't just think about him or erect a system of thought upon his life, they *believe* in him. This makes their human life meaningful or purposeful, and elevates their life beyond themselves.

3. Source and goal of humanity

The fault with the several human sciences is that they try to dictate to man what he should be. Modern man is badgered by the theories of psychologists, sociologists, anthropologists, and the social scientists. Helpful as they are, they have only fragmentary views or ideas of man to offer. They deal in ideas about man; they don't present that full and perfect image of man which is Christ. Christ is the only complete *source* and *goal* of humanity.

Crowds of people, said John the evangelist, ran to Christ and gathered around him: "he (Christ) set himself to teach them at some length." John had his reasons for pointing to Christ the Teacher of Life. The people of his day, as in ours, had many needs: food, sex, sleep, safety, growth, education, health. Jesus fulfills such needs with his acts of teaching, curing, feeding. Jesus does more than teach the goal of human life; he provides the means to attain it.

4. Gnostics and secularists

Perhaps the foremost danger John had to contend with in proclaiming Jesus and his message was something named Gnosticism, a very serious threat to Christianity. Gnostics were a peculiar lot, not too much different from the secularists and humanists speaking up today. Gnostics rejected revelation and its response, faith. They trusted entirely in the use of reason and other human means for solving human problems. Some of their teaching was so similar to the genuine Christian faith that it could easily fool the Christians. Our faith is tested in the same way by the many secular theories, ideals, and ideologies propagated about man. Without our Christian faith for a guide, we can't easily tell apart what's genuine and what's counterfeit about man.

John the evangelist didn't rout or overcome the Gnostics in his lifetime. Another Christian apologist defending humanity against them was St. Irenaeus of Lyons. He followed John in his concern for the truth about Christ and about man. Two of his famous and most quotable sayings are: "God became man in order that man might become God," and "The glory of God is man living fully."

5. The true man

How did Irenaeus understand man? Not as that two-part composition of body and soul as we usually do. With the Bible for his source of information, he thought of man three-dimensionally: man is body, soul, and spirit. The human soul is empowered with intellect and will, but the spirit enables man to be open to Christ and to the Spirit of God. Man's spirit is to be filled with Christ's spirit. The life of faith helps man to complete himself. So if he loses or lacks this life he loses or lacks likewise a part of his humanity. The true man is all three: body, soul, spirit.

Christ, John, Irenaeus, all three teach the truth about man. The truth will be difficult to practice, but at least it won't diminish or dwarf man. "God became man in order that man might become God." "The glory of God is man living fully." Christ said, "I am . . . the truth" (Jn 14:6), and he meant not only the truth about God but the truth about man as well. By not merely learning but contemplating his image, and letting him take over our lives, we'll be truthful to ourselves.

Seventeenth Sunday of the Year
2 K 4:42-44; Ep 4:1-6; Jn 6:1-15

Seeing This Sign

1. The case of Tommy

The mother of Tommy remembers his First Communion vividly. He was the last of her children, the one and only boy of the family. Tommy's mother, father, and sisters all got into the act of preparing him for the solemn event. The evening before, one of his sisters came running excitedly to her mother: "He's not ready, he's not ready, he believes like a Protestant; he thinks it's only a sign!"

That incident upset the whole house. Tommy was called before the catechetical board of the family to give an account of himself. After some prodding, it turned out the dialogue with his sister hinged upon an earlier event. Tommy had been watching TV programs picturing in clear childlike ways the human digestive system. He saw graphically how good food and drink are assimilated into the human body and bad are cast off or eliminated. When his mother tried to explain how we eat the body of Christ and drink his blood, Tommy, recalling the educational program, replied, "Why, that's ridiculous!"

Tommy was ready to accept the bread and wine as signs in memory of the Last Supper but not as containing the realities of the flesh and blood of Christ. Tommy's thinking was straightened out before morning, but surely not enough for him to understand the fine theological distinction between sign and reality.

Tommy's fascination with the sign-element of the Eucharist epitomizes the reaction to the signs with which Jesus tested the faith of his people. The Johannine gospel says they were "impressed by the signs he gave," and "seeing the sign" of the multiplication of the loaves and fishes they were about to make him their king.

2. One of seven signs

The multiplication is one of seven signs John selects from many others which support the theme and purpose of his gospel. For, his gospel features "signs" or symbols more than any other gospel.

The miraculous multiplication of the loaves and fishes serves his theme and purpose precisely. He calls it one of Jesus' signs since it points beyond itself to something else. In order to sharpen our understanding of this event, he awakes us to its symbolic character. This miracle is a wonderful work of God which reveals Jesus to his people, one sign among many revealing who Jesus is. More than a sign, the event combines the word and work of Jesus into a life-giving reality. Sign and reality are joined together here in an appeal for faith.

3. Its multiple sign-value

John sees the multiplication as a centerpiece on the table of divine generosity. Its meaning points both backward and forward in history. Two details seem to refer it to the Old Testament. First, the people are situated on a hillside, recalling the Old Testament scene of the Israelites gathered at Mt. Sinai. Secondly, the miracle is connected with the Passover feast, suggesting the feeding of the crowd during the Israelites' passover from Egypt to Chanaan.

Two other details orient the event toward the future event of the Last Supper, namely, the word-formula Jesus uses, almost identical with his at the Last Supper, and the fact that he alone distributes the food to the people. All such incidentals heighten the meaning of the original event.

Now, how does his version of the event affect us?

4. The sign of the Eucharist

Not having been among the crowd of five thousand fed by Christ, we can't relish the taste of the bread and fish. But what they signify, what they point to—the bread of life, the Eucharist—are impressive. The life of Christ is given and received under the visible signs of bread and wine. They contain and contribute the invisible reality of his life. Nobody can afford to boycott the Eucharist and still expect to nourish his day-to-day Christian life. Nobody can survive on Christ's words alone; his words are an invitation to accept the reality of his life. To receive the Eucharist is an act of thanksgiving in itself. We thank God for his gifts by eating at his table.

My plea, or the plea of the evangelist John, for the more frequent and more fervent reception of the Eucharist is nothing like a sales pitch. We leave it to Christ to substantiate our claims with the reality of his life. The sign of the Eucharist *is* the reality of his life.

5. Sacramental life

The early Christian writer Origen remarked about a story other than that of the multiplication yet applicable here, "Everything that is done, is done *in sacramentis*," that is, by means of signs. Divine life, so far as it comes to us through revelation, is incarnational. God is incarnated in Christ, Christ in his Church and his sacraments. The whole incarnation is a sign or, if you will, a sacrament. The law of sacramentality pervades the liturgy, the law by which we use signs in order to see and hear what is unseen and unheard, what contains and conveys an inward life, the life of grace.

The law of incarnation or sacramentality has two sources: the flesh-spirit nature of man and the Incarnate

Christ himself. We just can't have contact with God excepting through sensible realities. We Catholics don't believe bread and wine have any magical power. Yet they're full of spiritual meaning and power when employed by our great High Priest. As he incarnated his divine spirit in the body of Mary, so he incarnates his life in bread and wine. They become, through his omnipotent handling, the effective means of the Christian life.

Eighteenth Sunday of the Year
Ex 16:2-4, 12-15; Ep 4:17, 20-24; Jn 6:24-35

The Bread of Life

You may think this far-fetched, yet in a sense true—all
the bread we eat should be a reminder of the bread of the
Eucharist. If we were in dire need, if bread were the only
thing left between us and starvation, and if this bread
were supplied to us by God, we would be more inclined
to think of it as the gift of God and the staff of life.

1. Manna in the desert

Put yourself back in the times John wrote his gospel,
which was about 100 A.D. He tried to awaken in the
Hebrews an appreciation of the Eucharist through the
remembrance of the desert manna. John saw the manna
as type or sign of the Eucharist. It was, along with quail,
the food God furnished to the Hebrews emigrating from
Egypt. He took care of them in their time of need. For
John, manna served the same purpose as did the multiplication of the loaves and fishes, the sign we heard about
last Sunday. Both pointed to the spiritual food of the
Eucharist.

The Israelites, back in the days of their trek across the
Sinai peninsula, murmured against God and longed for
the good old days in Egypt when they had at least enough
food to eat. God quieted them down by sending them the
staple food of manna and quail. The quail was easily
caught while resting on its southbound flight, and the
manna, a honeydew substance that dropped from trees,
was picked up early each morning.

Manna, a godsend of staple food. Food becomes staple

when basic and necessary for life. By sending the Israelites their daily supply of food, God doesn't defy the law of supply and demand. His deal with them doesn't initiate a sort of welfare program. They still have to search and work for their food and drink. We wrongly interpret this desert scene if we picture the Israelites lumbering along to the promised land, lying idly by while God does everything for them but stuff the food into their mouths.

2. Bread for a journey

John the Evangelist takes Jesus at his word: he is the *bread of life*. As manna was the staple food for the Israelites—they ate it continually till they crossed the Canaan border, so is the Eucharist the staple food for Christians journeying to eternal life. The Eucharist too is a gift from God which "gives life to the world." That life is already a sampling of eternal life. John isn't saying we can take or leave it. No, he's emphatically asserting that without it we die an eternal death.

Moreover, Jesus is "the true bread" which comes down from heaven. Manna was a heavenly gift, Jesus is more so. Manna was eaten up to the Canaan border, not beyond it. The gift of "the true bread" will endure forever, endowed with the very life of Christ. What will the afterlife be like? Here is an indication—the life of Jesus will be the same, now and forever.

3. "I am"

The name Jesus gave himself supports the Johannine meaning: "I am the bread of life." The "I am" which John uses seven times in his gospel, harks back to Exodus 3:14, where God introduces himself to Moses as "I am who I Am." The God of the Old Testament is the one and only God, active among his people, their savior. He makes himself known to them by his generosity, faithfulness and power. Jesus is the same God who gives himself as the bread of life. Under the form of bread he becomes the source of life, the savior of mankind. "Yes, if you do not believe that I am he, you will die in your sins" (Jn 8:24).

The reason we should take John's gospel as addressed to ourselves and not simply to his contemporaries is that their situation is the same as ours. They hadn't seen or met Jesus in person. That's why John's intention was to show how Jesus is present in our communities by word and sacrament. We come in contact with him through sacramental life.

4. Break bread together

Bread and wine are only part of the Eucharistic symbolism. Just as meaningful is the *breaking* of bread *together*. The original name for the Eucharist is "the breaking of bread." Because it's meant to be shared, the bread is broken and the cup of wine passed along to everyone gathered at the table. We eat and drink together in an act of fellowship. Ours is a friendship meal. Despite our frictions, disagreements, quarrels, enmities, Christ reconciles us.

God offers the gift of his life; he makes the first move, he invites. The wise thing for us is to accept his invitation. To refuse is to lead "the aimless kind of life that pagans live." Men who look only to this life to find their fulfillment are filled with "illusory desires." Since they refuse to give up their old way of life, their old self, their life will end in utter disappointment. It leaves behind a bitter taste.

5. Gift of wisdom

John portrays Jesus as Wisdom personified. You'll never go hungry or thirsty if you eat and drink of the life of Wisdom. "Come and eat my bread, drink the wine I have prepared! Leave your folly and you will live, walk in the ways of perception" (Pr 9:5-6). "Approach me, you who desire me, and take your fill of my fruits" (Si 24:19).

The bread of life is a gift, not a handout. We still have to *work* for the food that endures to eternal life. The life and work of the faith prepare us for it. The more we guard against the illusory desires of our senses, the more we deny ourselves, the more we relinquish our attachments, the more God fills us with his life.

Nineteenth Sunday of the Year
1 K 19:4-8; Ep 4:30-5:2; Jn 6:41-51

Rejection

1. Anti-feelings

A symptom of our age, of its spirit, is the frequent use of the word "anti." Compound words are made with it to denote anyone or anything "against" or "opposite." Antidote, antifreeze, antipathy, antiseptic, etc. Some people, critical and negative-minded, are simply called in informal speech "antis." They reject a particular practice, policy, party, etc. Oftentimes they have no positive suggestions to make.

Not everyone or everything anti is bad or evil. There are, however, many anti-feelings, which generally are bad and cause much harm. Feelings of dislike, hatred, rejection, are harmful. Take child abuse or neglect. Why do some parents yell at, scold, punch, hit, and yank their child? Because they feel anti. They take their anti-feelings out on their child.

2. Elijah

All three biblical readings present cases of anti-feeling or rejection. The first case concerns Elijah, victimized by the notorious Tyrian princess, Jezebel, queen-wife of Ahab, king of Israel. Elijah battles with the queen over the introduction and spread of the Canaanite religion in Israel. Jezebel fosters this foreign religion, the worship of the agricultural god, Baal, among the Israelites. She has a gang of false prophets to help her along. The Israelites, an agricultural people, are attracted to Baal in order to win from him the blessing of fertile lands. Thus Baalism threatens to oust the religion and worship of the one true God and to become the national religion and way of life.

Elijah, a prophetic revolutionary, appeals to the national conscience against Jezebel and incurs her wrath. He argues that no trade advantages with the Phoenicians should open the way to paganism. No domestic good is worth the infiltration of false worship and religion. Elijah dares taking a stand against the evils of his government.

For this reaction to her pet scheme, Jezebel rejects Elijah and drives him out of the country. Poor Elijah then enters a fugitive life.

He deserves our sympathy. We all fear rejection. We all feel deserving of respect, if not of love. Some of us, especially the young and tender-hearted, are crushed by rejection and never fully recover. Some, feeling the need to be accepted and loved, are hurt irremediably. Rejection cuts to the quick; it leaves a permanent scar.

Rejection may not be so total as Elijah experienced it. Milder forms are harmful too. Bearing a grudge is a form of rejection, so is losing one's temper at another, shouting abusively at somebody, raising a fuss unnecessarily, name-calling, and dealing with another in spite, or revenge. Such "rejection slips" never seem so offensive until we ourselves receive them.

Elijah reacts typically for one who has been rejected. He takes to flight and feels terribly lonely. He even has the death-wish. What else is he to do in the face of King Ahab's accusation: "So there you are, you scourge of Israel?" What else when Queen Jezebel swears by her gods to do him in? What else when the faithless Israelites do the splits in homage to both Yahweh and Baal?

Elijah does what any normal religious-minded man would do if driven into loneliness by his fellowmen. Unable to find comfort and strength among men, he seeks it from God. First of all, he's sustained by the food and drink God supplies, which is enough to carry him over to Mt.

Horeb. Then he meets with God and discovers that God isn't the loneliness of man. Rather, God is a silence and presence. That presence is for Elijah, as for everyone, a source of peace and courage, and a sign of divine acceptance. The very name of Elijah signifies his faith and trust in that presence: "My God is Yahweh."

3. Jesus

Jesus too experiences rejection by his countrymen after telling them, "I am the bread that came down from heaven." The only way they have to know him is to judge him by his family background. Naturally, full of complaint about him, they reject belief in him as the Messiah and Lord. Who must this "son of Joseph" think himself to be? How can he claim a heavenly origin? They know his father and mother. Their questioning his identity has a note of sarcasm in it.

Their anti-feeling doesn't prevent Jesus from offering them and all his followers the bread of his life and love. Elijah takes refuge to the presence of God on Mt. Horeb; Jesus takes up his presence in the Eucharist, to be among the people he loves and lays down his life for. Scorned by the Jewish religious leaders, Jesus could have withdrawn from human society; he could have become the lonely outcast, the loveless reject. Instead, he establishes that loving presence among men which remains to this day a sign of his acceptance. Jesus once tented among men; he now tabernacles in their midst.

God in Christ considers all men worthy of his love and acceptance. His presence in the Eucharist gives proof of it. He rejects no one who comes to him with a contrite heart.

Do we love and accept others only to the degree that we love ourselves in them? Or do we love the ideal of ourselves in them? Must we first refer to ourselves before we can love and accept them? Should they fail us or express anti-feelings toward us, the Eucharistic Lord enables us with his presence, his love, his acceptance to reject no one.

Solemnity of the Assumption of Mary
1 Ch 15:3-4, 15, 16; 16:1-2; 1 Cor 15:54-57; Lk 11:27-28

Honour Your Mother

1. A child's story

I asked the children in one of the CCD classes to write a biblical story as a home assignment. They were supposed to use a biblical setting and weave their story imaginatively around it, without repeating anything further out of the Bible. One of the girls spun a story she called "The Cradle."

The story has to do with Jesus, Mary and Joseph, and Joseph's sister Victoria who has a baby boy. The announcement of his birth gladdens their hearts. Over the dinner table they discuss what each will bring the baby boy as a birthday present. Mary decides to sew him a green outfit, "with a hat and booties." Joseph is going to make a box to hold the baby's possessions. Jesus doesn't know what to make, but at breakfast the next morning he asks Joseph if he can borrow his tools. Later the same day, Mary comes to the shed and finds Jesus busy but not yet ready to leave for Victoria's. So Mary and Joseph leave without him.

Toward evening, Mary starts to worry about Jesus just as he walks in with a cradle, all varnished and pillowed, under his arm. Mary and Joseph are proud of Jesus. Victoria puts her child into the cradle.

2. Happy the womb

This was the child's story in short. Aside from being a quaint work of the imagination, it gave a true picture of the Hebrew love of children, of their joy over the birth of

a child, and their family spirit. In the book of Proverbs
we read the wishful prayer: "May you be the joy of your
father, the gladness of her who bore you" (23:25). Jacob's
wife Leah, after having received the birth of a second son
from her slave-girl, exclaimed, "What happiness! Women
will call me happy!" (Gn 30:13). When Mary paid her
relative Elizabeth a visit, Elizabeth recognized Mary to be
with child: "Of all women you are the most blessed, and
blessed is the fruit of your womb" (Lk 1:42).

Elizabeth's cry is repeated by the woman who listened
to Jesus speaking with authority to the crowd: "Happy the
womb that bore you and the breasts you sucked!" In
Mary's womb, truly, the Word of God, Jesus, was formed
into flesh, modeled into the image and likeness of God.
Mary nursed him, fondled him in her arms, clothed, fed,
and raised him up into manhood. Humanly speaking, in
their home at Nazareth, he was given an education of character such as no one else has received from a mother.

3. Hear the word

Did Jesus then somehow slight or dishonor his mother
in his reply to the anonymous woman admirer? No, he
wasn't denying how happy she was over his birth; he was
simply stating how preferable it is to hear the word of God
and keep it. That is, a blood relationship doesn't guarantee
salvation. To live by the word of God is to belong to God's
family.

In point of fact, Mary could and did rejoice on both
counts. At the angelic announcement that she was to become the mother of Jesus, she thought over the announcement and wondered about it (Lk 1:29). After his birth,
and after the visit from the shepherds, "As for Mary, she
treasured all these things and pondered them in her heart"
(Lk 2:19). After Jesus as a young boy was lost and returned from Jerusalem, "His mother stored up all these
things in her heart" (Lk 2:51). Mary wasn't only a mother

to Jesus, she took the events of his life and his message to heart.

4. Close associates

The association of his life with hers was more than coincidental. He honored her with the immaculate conception and bodily assumption, two privileges that stand out at the start and finish of her human existence, two privileges "most closely bound to one another." In consequence of keeping her free from original sin, he didn't subject her to the law of bodily corruption in the grave. "She did not have to wait until the end of time for the redemption of her body" (*Munificentissimus Deus*, encyclical letter of Pope Pius XII).

Jesus and Mary are most intimately associated on Calvary. He has yet to die in her presence, but through his death he wins the victory over her death. Her "death is swallowed up in (his) victory." The assumption of Mary is the crown and completion of their life together, the last and absolute honor Jesus bestows upon his mother. The two are reunited in their heavenly home, she to share with her Son a happy, perfect life.

In 1950, a quarter-century ago, Pope Pius XII declared the assumption of Mary a dogma of the Church, and predicted her privilege would "contribute in no small way to the advantage of human society," and then pointed out three advantages that would accrue from it.

5. Our advantages

The first is that it would offer "a new incentive to piety toward her (Mary)." We ought to address her, "Pray for us sinners now and at the hour of our death," so that she will obtain for us earthly consolations and peace, and lead us into the glory of heaven.

The dogma of Mary's assumption came shortly after

World War II, when anti-humanistic policies and practices had showed themselves. Pope Pius XII hoped we
might be "more and more convinced of the value of a
human life entirely devoted to the heavenly Father's will
and to bringing good to others." Mary's life was an indescribable sacrament, signifying and realizing the value of
the life of Jesus, God and man.

The final advantage to come to us from this solemnity
is that it "will make our belief in our own resurrection
stronger and render it more effective." Jesus valued the
bodily life of his mother so much as to spare her, by the
power of his resurrection, the corruption of the grave. By
his resurrection and her assumption, Jesus will deliver us
from the grave. "So let us thank God for giving us the
victory through our Lord Jesus Christ."

Twentieth Sunday of the Year
Pr 9:1-6; Ep 5:15-20; Jn 6:51-58

Prudence

1. Invitation to a feast

What will you have? A full course dinner or a diet of bread and water? The question sounds as if it came from a waitress in a restaurant. Actually, it was suggested by the reading from the book of proverbs, a piece of wisdom literature from the Old Testament. There wisdom appears as a grand hostess inviting everyone to a sumptuous banquet. To be wise, to be prudent, to be tactful is like sitting down to a feast of food and drink.

This way of thinking may be a bit foreign to our mentality, and yet we imply and come close to it in our way of acting. The ancient Hebrews thought too much wine-bibbing an abuse; wine drinking should lead to happy get-togethers and a songfest. Nowadays many people smoke pot, take drugs, and blow their minds with drink. They intend in so doing to reach a realm of life otherwise closed to them. They seek a full, happy life by false ways and means.

2. Prudence or foolishness

There are, basically, two antithetical influences upon human life, two ways of living, two invitations to life in this world—prudent and foolish, right and wrong, good and evil. Wisdom or prudence guides one way, foolishness another. Every choice we make, every decision, every judgment goes either one way or the other—prudent or foolish. We make such choices or judgments hundreds of times a day. Some are so important they determine the course of life forever.

"So be very careful about the sort of lives you lead, like intelligent and not like senseless people. This may be a wicked age, but your lives should redeem it. And do not be thoughtless . . . be filled with the Spirit."

How senseless, thoughtless of us to make weighty decisions without due consideration. Jumping to conclusions, making snap judgments, acting on the spur of the moment —all such are acts of imprudence. They mess up lives.

What makes people opt for a bread-and-butter, starvation diet instead of a well-balanced meal? What makes them imprudent? Here are three examples of indiscretions, imprudences.

3. Three imprudences

"Walk in the ways of perception," says the wise man. The ways of perception are impossible to walk with eyes closed. Among us, at times, are people with closed minds. They adopt a know-it-all attitude. Their minds run in one gear, unable to shift according to the situation. They may blink at the changes that sweep by them. Or close their eyes fully to reality. Their good intentions and meaning well are insufficient. Prudence is the only way out of their self-deception.

Or take the people who look at the truth of reality, but nearsightedly. They consider and judge concrete reality entirely too narrowly, from their own viewpoint, too subjectively. Through cunning, conniving or scheming they may outdo others. Their diplomacy or wizardry hardly rates the name of prudence. Whatever works for their own advantage appears to be the useful thing to do, the pragmatic thing in the greedy pursuit of self-gratifying goals. Money, property, whatever advances them or improves their status is their standard of judgment. They make deals with their consciences.

A third kind of imprudence is that which hesitates to act out of fear. It may be slow to consider, moderate in judgment, but neglectful to act. It holds back timidly, for fear of making a mistake. If irresolute, if never one to "make up my mind," it may be that I try too hard to shun all danger.

4. A balanced diet

Prudence is the only virtue that offers man a balanced diet. It strikes the right balance between extremes; it puts human life in order. A prudent man is a good man. An order of rank exists among the virtues, and prudence is the foremost of them. "All virtue is necessarily prudent," says St. Thomas Aquinas. Prudence is the standard or measure of all goodness. Without it, the Ten Commandments are impossible to keep. Sin is a transgression of the Ten Commandments, and every sin is an act of imprudence. Prudence is a guide for the application of the Commandments to concrete human action.

Practically speaking, prudence is identifiable with conscience, that duty to judge objectively the concrete reality of human life. Conscience has to do with the ways and means toward the Christian goal of life. Every human act leads either to or away from that goal. The function of prudence is to deliberate over the aspects of a situation, to judge the course of action, and to command what to do. Prudence not only *knows* what is what but *does* what is what. Down-to-earth realities are its concern, the field of its operation.

5. Seeking advice

Sometimes, before making decisions that can make or break us, we turn to a friend for advice. A true and tried friend, and a prudent one at that, can help us to see into a concrete problem more objectively. "Teach each other, and advise each other, in all wisdom," says St. Paul (Col 3:16).

In matters affecting eternal life one has no wiser friend to consult than the Eucharistic Lord. He gives the wine of wisdom and the bread of teaching together with his flesh and blood. Wisdom is manifest in the man of prudent action. The prudent Christ alerts him, through his Spirit, to the opportunity of grace and inspires him to do God's will. His flesh and blood are the food and drink of wisdom.

Twenty-first Sunday of the Year
Jos 24:1-2, 15-17, 18; Ep 5:21-32; Jn 6:60-69

United in Christ

1. Apostasy, heresy, schism

Three words have all but dropped out of the Catholic vocabulary. You have to look for them in the catechisms, dictionaries, and encyclopedias. We could play a guessing game here, to see whether you can name them. But not to keep you curious any longer, here they are: apostasy, heresy, and schism. Who sees them in print or hears of them nowadays?

Why aren't they in vogue? Is it that the realities of apostasy, heresy, and schism no longer occur? Or that the official Church doesn't bother to bring such formal charges against anyone? Or, finally, is the situation in the Church so chaotic and confused as to make it virtually impossible to detect apostates, heretics, and schismatics?

The fact is that similar phenomena, under different labels, are found in our society. Think of desertion, divorce, deportation, defection, draft-dodging, secession. They occur elsewhere in a society, then why not in the Church?

2. What they mean

To refresh our memories, let us see what the three mean. Apostasy is definable as the rejection of the Catholic faith or religion. An apostate is one who breaks away from the Church. Heresy is the acceptance of and persistence in beliefs contrary to the true doctrine of the Church. A heretic is one who disbelieves an essential point of Catholic doctrine. Schism is a party separation due to failure to recognize all Catholic doctrine or to submit to papal authority. A schismatic is one who belongs to a separatist group.

3. In history

The three names have a centuries-old history. The first, apostasy, is dated as far back as Old Testament history. Ancient Israel had its share of apostates. The temptation to apostasy arose whenever the Israelites consorted with foreign peoples who worshipped pagan gods. The Israelites were strongly attracted to Baal, the god of agriculture and fertility. They saw the great and good things done for them by Yahweh, and still they fell into idolatry.

Their belief in the one true God gave them unity. So did the capable leadership of Moses, Joshua, and the prophets. Joshua was the mediator of the covenant renewal. Under him, and at the religious center of Shechem, the Israelites promised, "We have no intention of deserting Yahweh and serving other gods!" They didn't always keep their promise.

Christ wasn't even finished with his life and teaching when disciples deserted him. "After this (after he preached the doctrine of the Eucharist to them), many of his disciples left him and stopped going with him." Christ was speaking "intolerable language" but was unwilling to compromise or water down his doctrine for the purpose of retaining his disciples. He gave Peter and the other apostles the option of leaving him. This confrontation occasioned Peter's famous confession of faith and the question, "Lord, who shall we go to?"

Part of the traditional Christian catechesis was to warn against heresy since the teachings of Christ didn't have time to settle in men's minds and solidify there. The danger was so subtle that Paul spoke out against it even when others missed its implications. And the apostle Jude attacked heretics who still belonged to the Christian community, undermining the Christian life and belief. Heresy worked like a fifth column in the early Church.

4. Crises today

This last fact suggests a clue to our own crisis of faith. The sometimes confused thinking and chaotic behavior in the Church distort the categories of apostasy, heresy, and schism. No schismatic groups are breaking away from the Church and starting churches of their own. Nor is there *open* and *total* apostasy as sometimes happened in past centuries. Nor does the Church publicly censure doctrine as heresy. Anything wrong in the Church is kept much more secret, underground, partial, in the fringe or marginal areas, on the extreme right and the extreme left.

Of course, then, the drift away from orthodoxy is harder to detect. Doctrinal novelties, selfish interests, false teaching are less noticeable and not put down at once. A safe but long-range diagnosis of the failure of faith is this— the truth will come out, eventually. Christ assuredly won't let his Church fail entirely, though he may let it be afflicted with its own sores for a while, before he comes with his Spirit to its rescue.

5. Together in faith

The three—apostasy, heresy, schism—have this much in common: they disrupt the unity of the faith. And that disunity we do experience at the present time. In contrast to it is that other experience of the faith, namely, its cohesive force. In the midst of a crisis, we're experiencing more poignantly this thing together, how we belong to one another, our common responsibility. Just as the guilt of apostasy may involve a whole people, so does the strength of faith upbuild and unite us all.

One symbol for this unity is marriage. The marriage of Yahweh and Israel, the marriage of Christ and his Church.

Christ loved, sacrificed himself for the Church "to make her holy." The Church submits herself to Christ in love and obedience.

Perhaps our unity in Christ is less apparent than we should like it to be. Perhaps we're not giving "way to one another in obedience to Christ" as we should. The forces of disruption are secretly at work in the Church, sometimes under the guise of pluralism and diversity. Just as forcefully is Christ caring for his Church, for its unity. "Lord, who shall we go to?"

Twenty-second Sunday of the Year
Dt 4:1-2, 6-8; Jm 1:17-18, 21-22, 27; Mk 7:1-8, 14-15, 21-23

Piety and Conduct

1. Cry contamination

Sitting down to eat with unwashed hands recalls my boyhood days. What boy or girl hasn't tried it? Who of us in our childhood days wasn't examined for clean hands and elbows, on a matter of cleanliness and courtesy? The unclean practice of Christ's followers, to which the Pharisees objected, was something else again. They were supposed to wash themselves to remove any contamination from contact with Gentile peoples.

Jesus took issue with the Pharisees over this point of purification. They were a very exclusive religious group—the Separated Ones they were called. One-sided and legalistic, they kept aloof from Gentiles, sinners, and less-observant Jews in fear of contamination.

They also made life unbearable with their unwritten traditions, elaborate interpretations of the law of Moses. Jesus brought out the disproportion between minor infractions, like that of ceremonial washing, and the neglect of primary things. So many little things we do, he said in effect, became routine and automatic. Life and meaning have gone out of them through practice.

2. Commandments come first

In short, the Pharisees pushed the wrong priorities. Jesus put first things first, which were the commandments of God. For those who kept them, they were the source of life. They were saving laws, like the stars at night that guided sailors safely to their destination. Given to man by the Father of all light, the creator of the stars, they were beacons lighting up the way of salvation. Obedience to the commandments demonstrated Israel's wisdom and understanding. The commandments inculcated the wisdom to know the goal of life and to employ the means toward it. By keeping them, Israel shone like a star of example to other nations.

You know the poor Pharisees are always getting it in the neck from us latter-day Christians. Not all of them were as narrow-minded as they appear in the gospel. The accusations against them, for their faults, should be taken as warnings to us. How much better are we if we misinterpret the commandments of God in one or other of the two following ways?

3. Splitting the difference

The first way to falsify God's commandments is to set up our own priorities. We keep those congenial to us, we neglect others. Some feel the imperative of the first and third commandments, those requiring the worship of God and the keeping of the Sabbath. They wouldn't think of absenting themselves from Sunday worship, because that would be an enormous sin. But they think little of abusing the divine name or cheating their neighbor or stealing or being unfaithful to their spouse. On the other hand, there are those who miss Sunday worship without qualms of conscience—they consider worshippers hypocritical—and yet pride themselves on observing the rest of the commandments.

What's wrong with these two attitudes? They split the commandments down the middle. They take sides, separating unduly the outward and the inward observance of the divine law. *Doers* of some laws and *hearers* only of others. Against the first group Jesus says: "This people honours me only with lip-service, while their hearts are far from me. The worship they offer is worthless." Whereas the non-worshippers are no better off: "For it is from within, from men's hearts, that evil intentions emerge. . . All these evil things come from within and make a man unclean." The clean observance of the divine law counts for nothing if it proceeds from unclean intentions.

4. Leveling down

A second Pharisaic way of acting levels down all law, divine and human, serious and slight, to the same importance. The Pharisees were wrong in teaching that the law of Moses, 613 prescriptions in all, were to be kept in all detail as if they were the complete and valid expression of God's will. We do the same whenever we "put aside the commandments of God to cling to human traditions," whenever the doctrines we teach are only human regulations. We, indeed, do worse by setting human and civil law above divine and church law. A secularistic, materialistic society that knows and acknowledges no law but its own cuts itself off from the divine presence, the source of spiritual light and life.

The essential fault with these two reactions to the divine commandments is their mathematics. They subtract the outward from the inward observance instead of adding the two. Or they add human laws to the divine without subtracting them in value. The truly religious man keeps them both, the outward and the inward, the divine and the human, in the right priority.

5. Religion and practice

All I have said may seem to go against St. James' definition of "pure, unspoilt religion," which is to help widows and orphans and to keep oneself "uncontaminated by the world." St. James isn't giving a full definition of religion but promoting a practice without which religion is meaningless. We must help the needy, whoever they are. Aid to others shouldn't interfere with our duty to God, and vice versa. We ought to test piety and conduct with each other. True piety shows up in good conduct, and good conduct confirms true piety.

We church people have to be on our guard against the superficiality of much professed belief, or else we leave ourselves open to the charge of hypocrisy. A young New Yorker, a pop artist who uses ink-drawings in the style of Pogo and Peanuts, hits hard at hypocritical faith and religion. Two of his cartoon characters, geometric figures in the shape of the sun and a watermelon, are dialoguing over the theme of our liturgy. Mr. Sun is in need and cries for help. Mr. Watermelon just repeats religious formulas. Finally, Mr. Sun in exasperation says, "Could you forget the religion and help me?"

Twenty-third Sunday of the Year
Is 35:4-7; Jm 2:1-5; Mk 7:31-37

The Divine Economy

1. The messianic age

The title and subject-matter of this homily conjure up the picture of God the Economist, as though he were the regulator of world trade or of international business. In that economic sense God isn't at the head of a thrifty management, nor does he promote prosperity. The Fathers of the Church spoke of a divine economy because they saw in the world a divine plan for man.

The divine economy so managed world events that one age in particular was to be an age of prosperity. The messianic age—the people of the Old Testament were promised it. Isaiah, among others, announced it, and part of his announcement we read today. We also read in Mark something about its fulfillment, for Mark implicitly refers to Isaiah 35:6. Christ did "all things well," hence he must be the Messiah, the people thought.

Naturally, we all pay attention to the rise and fall of the economy, detecting signs of inflation or depression or recession. So did the Hebrew people look for signs of the divine economy. One sign was the cure of the blind, the deaf, the lame, the dumb. Another was an abundant water supply. When man was restored to health and mother earth was made fertile, happy days were theirs again.

2. The divine equality

What pleased the Hebrews about their God was that he showed no favoritism, that he was an impartial judge.

"Rich and poor are found together, Yahweh has made them all" (Pr 22:2). ". . . for he causes his sun to rise on bad men as well as good, and his rain to fall on honest and dishonest men alike" (Mt 5:45). The divine economy indicated to the Hebrews that their God had a sense of balanced judgment, of equality.

What would happen to us were we to copy the divine economy, to put into practice its principles? We should not have to prefer the well-dressed to the shabbily-dressed (for the difference in social rank between the rich and the poor is visible in their appearance). Our own economy would be the steadier. We would be rid of discrimination, prejudice, bias, snobbery, status-seeking.

3. A divided society

At a glance we see what's happening in our society. To some extent the rich are becoming wealthier, the poor becoming poorer. This isn't the total imbalance. Nor is segregation the whole story. We have many distinctions of class, color, and creed. Equal job and pay and federal aid opportunities are closed to many because of sex bias, anti-religious prejudices.

Resentment flares up among those who feel themselves pushed around, the economically and socially oppressed. Both are afflicted with speech impediments. The discriminating refuse to hear or speak to the discriminated. And the discriminated feel themselves so alienated from the discriminating they lisp or stutter in their presence. How are we to get out of this social impasse?

4. Double standard

The Bible puts its finger on the sore spot. Ours is a double standard of judgment, one for the haves, another for the have-nots. Our worldly standards are opposed to heavenly standards. Jesus and his teaching of the equality of peoples are our liberation. Jesus healed the unfortunate, removed their physical defects which were taken to be discriminatory. He went out of his way to help the "poor according to the world." He discovered them rich in faith. "How happy are the poor in spirit; theirs is the kingdom of heaven," he said (Mt 5:3).

We still live in the messianic era promised to the Hebrews. But through our own fault we live at the same time with discriminatory practices. They won't be easy to eradicate. The symptoms rest on the surface of our society; their roots lie deeper. The cure will come about as soon as we just don't demand our rights but also give up the wrongs benefiting us. Two wrongs don't make a single right.

5. Rash judgment

Discrimination, prejudice, bias—all are classifiable under rash judgment. They go against the universality of Christian love. When they surface and spread in a society, when such judgments lead to practices, they involve injustice.

Divine charity demands that we revise our judgments about the people we think beneath us. If the divine economy tolerates no divine discrimination, our human misjudgments must be out of order too. Not just in the big discriminations and biases we hear so much about, but in the little ones also. How much do we misjudge others by first impressions, by their looks, their mannerisms, their handicaps? Jesus asks, "Why do you observe the splinter in your brother's eye and never notice the plank in your own?" (Mt 7:3).

6. Equal justice

Moreover, discriminations and biases that keep men, women, and children from equal job, pay, and federal aid opportunities are violations against justice, which demands redress. In a word, restitution, which we hear of altogether too seldom nowadays. Yet, without equal justice in this world, we can talk about charity till we're blue in the face, without results.

Jesus did things particularly well for the poor. He deemed himself one of their number. One biblical commentator puts it this way: "As we believe in the *hidden* glory of Christ, so we must respect the *hidden* worth of the poor." Poor in money, rich in faith—their hidden worth.

Twenty-fourth Sunday of the Year
Is 50:4-9; Jm 2:14-18; Mk 8:27-35

Destined to Suffer

1. I believe

The great French novelist, Francois Mauriac, didn't
hesitate to describe in his novels the seamy side of life.
Read his *Viper's Tangle* or *Woman of the Pharisees* and
you'll grow heartsick at the sight of the ugly. And yet
Mauriac wasn't pessimistic about life. At the age of 84,
before he died, he said: "I believe . . . that life has meaning, a direction, a value; that no suffering is lost, that every
tear counts, each drop of blood. . ."

The first noteworthy thing about this wise old man's
observation about life is his profession of belief. He didn't
say, "I know, I feel certain, I'm of the opinion;" he said
rather, "I believe. . ." That life has meaning, direction,
value would be well nigh impossible to establish if we
didn't believe it.

2. Every tear, each drop

Suffering and death have raised for many people the
question of the meaninglessness of life. If God exists, and
he's as good, loving, and merciful as they say he is, why
should he permit the evil of suffering ending in death? In
response to such a complaint, which is quite common,
Mauriac's testimony sounds startling indeed.

But Mauriac is saying much more, without exaggera-
tion. ". . . *no* suffering is lost . . . *every* tear counts . . . *each*
drop of blood. . ." He can make this assertion only on
condition that faith gives value to suffering and makes

every tear and blood drop count. Suffering, accepted in a
spirit of faith, is a good work. "Faith is like that: if good
works do not go with it, it is quite dead." Of all the works
of faith, suffering seems to be the most intolerable but is
the most convincing.

3. God suffers and dies

God reveals his love and fidelity to us precisely through
his own suffering and death. They may seem to turn us
against him but, paradoxically, he couldn't produce better
evidence of his love and sacrifice than in Christ. Like a
good loving parent that doesn't satisfy every whim and
fancy of a child, that doesn't lavish on a child all the good
things of this world, God adds to the beauty and glory and
joy of his creation the gift of himself. He demands suffering and death of himself no less than of his people.

The lesson of divine suffering and death is taught in the
two readings from Isaiah and Mark, which complement
each other. The Isaian reading is a song about the servant
who doesn't spare himself suffering. "I offered my back to
those who struck me, my cheeks to those who tore at my
beard; I did not cover my face against insult and spittle."
The servant accepts suffering willingly, not grudgingly.
He serves by suffering.

Mark in using the title of the "Son of Man" has the
suffering servant in mind. "The Son of Man was destined
to suffer grievously." Note that this statement comes after
Peter confesses his faith in the Messiah. The messianic
mission Jesus has is to suffer and die. God suffers and dies
in the only way possible for him, the only way he knows
how—in the human life of his Son. It would be unthinkable
of God if he found something utterly contradictory to or
unworthy of himself in suffering and death.

4. His destiny is ours

The destiny of Christ is to suffer and die. On more than

one occasion he slips through the grasp of his enemies and eludes his destiny. The destiny willed by his Father is his personal choice. And he in turn wills the same destiny for man: "If anyone wants to be a follower of mine, let him renounce himself and take up his cross and follow me."

Destiny in this context must be given a special meaning, which has nothing to do with inescapable fate. Christ, because destined to suffer, is defined as Savior. His suffering and death have saving value for others. The same destiny applies to his followers. Their life is defined by a co-destiny with his. Destiny then expresses the divine intention for man, what man is to be, the accomplishment of a life.

5. If I want

Destiny doesn't leave out of human life the fact of openness, freedom, willingness. Christ makes this very clear: "If anyone *wants* to be. . ." Some people go through life thinking everything is determined for them. They feel themselves thrust into a slot from which they can't wiggle out. They usually blame their environment—if only that were better, how much better off they would be!

In reality human life is open to numerous possibilities, and at no stage of it is man unable to change his direction, revise his values, opt for a new meaning. His life is restive and unfinished until he breathes his last. Up to that moment, each of us can make a new start, each of us can say to himself, "If I want to be a follower of Christ, I can—now."

6. The science of the cross

What Mauriac believed in, what is proposed to us in the liturgical readings, is beautifully exemplified in the life, suffering, and death of Edith Stein, a Jewish convert to the faith. When Edith, an up-and-coming philosopher, applied for entrance to the Carmel of Cologne, the superior there hesitated to take in someone who still had work to do in the world. She reminded Edith that she couldn't continue her intellectual work in the convent. Edith answered: "It is not human activity that can help us but the Passion of Christ. It is a share in that that I desire."

Her desire was fulfilled later. When imprisoned near Amersfoort, and before being taken into a concentration camp, she penned a note to her superior: "One can only learn a *Scientia Crucis* if one feels the Cross in one's own person. I was convinced of this from the very first and have said with all my heart: *Ave crux, spes unica!*"

Twenty-fifth Sunday of the Year
Ws 2:17-20; Jm 3:16-4:3; Mk 9:30-37

War and Peace

1. Billions in armaments

In 1963, when Pope John XXIII published his encyclical "Peace on Earth," the United Nations reported that governments spent $120 billion annually on armaments. The amount was 8-9% of that spent on the world's goods and services, and two-thirds of the annual income of under-developed countries.

The statistics haven't changed noticeably. The U.S.—to take one example—spends in the neighborhood of $70 billion on military manpower, weapons, upkeep, etc. We hear speculation about how peace is more profitable than war. The long-awaited peace hasn't shown any big dividends for social priorities. Ruthless, unprincipled men are still wheeling and dealing in the lives of their fellowmen.

2. True causes of war

Our past experience in war teaches anyone with the wisdom to observe that the true causes of war aren't money or profit. War is a human contrivance, springing from human jealousy and ambition. The Bible which points to such causes, speaks from experience. Bible history is riddled with the reports of war. One nation won't be outdone by another, and in order to curb ambition one nation makes might its right over another. Ancient Israel was caught more than once in the crossfire between nations of the east and the west.

To those who maintained total disarmament was im-

possible, and that the only way to peace was by an equality of arms, Pope John declared that "the true and solid
peace of nations consists . . . but in mutual trust alone"
(#113). So long as arms are at hand, people will live in
fear and expectation of war. Trust has to grow out of an
inner conviction, said Pope John.

In speaking of peace, biblical wisdom sees it coming
to those who are kindly, considerate, compassionate, helpful, impartial, and sincere. James says the wisdom that
makes for peace has no "trace of partiality or hypocrisy
in it." Jealousy and ambition, the two causes of war, are
equivalent to partiality and hypocrisy. Wherever we find
the least partiality and hypocrisy there is bound to be dis-
harmony.

Now, of course, Mr. Average Man, however Christian
he may be, feels himself helpless against the juggernaut
of those who profit from war. He feels like a dove in a nest
of hawks. The godless test and torture the virtuous. We
have seen this happen in the case of conscientious objection and the suspicion of ethnics (the confinement of
Japanese nationals during World War II).

3. Minor disharmonies

But the problem of war and peace on an international
scale doesn't excuse any one of us from applying the biblical wisdom to ourselves. How many of our minor disharmonies—the quarrels and bickerings—don't arise from the
same causes? Jealousy and ambition. Are we organized
within ourselves for war or peace? Can we truly consider
ourselves peave-loving sons of God and not treat others
kindly, considerately, compassionately, helpfully, impar-
tially, and sincerely.

Our minor disharmonies strike us more poignantly on
hearing about the contention of the apostles over top-
ranking position. One would think people so close to
Christ would be more selfless and inambitious. But not so.

The Master has to set a child in their midst for an example. A child is dependent upon the service of his elders. So the apostles are to serve rather than to be served.

4. Peace for progress

Will we ever learn that not the competitiveness of war but peace prepares for progress? Think this over. You often hear the argument that science and technology advance by leaps and bounds in a time of war? Is this really true? If you weigh the war casualties, military and civilian, the destruction of land and property against the so-called progress in time of war, aren't we fooling ourselves?

Only a recognizable man of peace like Pope John can be a peacemaker. One of the last acts of his pontificate, his last will and legacy several months before his death, was to issue his encyclical on peace. It came not only when the world was war-torn but the UN was in crisis.

5. The argument for peace

His argument for peace runs as follows. God fixed order into the material universe so as to have it running smoothly—the sun, moon, stars, and planets operating in unison, the seasons regulating human life. Similarly he instilled order in human beings. The human rights with which he endowed them establish a common *bond*. Human rights tend inexorably and inevitably to a common *cause* even beyond barriers. Rights common to man are apt to meet with universal response. Corresponding to the rights are duties.

Pope John saw four duties establishing the order among men: "an order founded on truth, built according to justice, vivified and integrated by charity, and put in practice in freedom" (#167).

A man characteristically optimistic, Pope John wasn't so visionary as to foresee peace attainable by human effort alone. Peace is the gift of God in Christ: "help from on high is necessary," he said (#168). "For he (Christ) is the peace between us. . . Later he came to bring the good news of peace, peace to you who were far away and peace to those who were near at hand" (Ep 2:14, 17). We pray along with Pope John that the rulers of peoples, and we ourselves, "may guarantee and defend the great gift of peace" (#171).

Twenty-sixth Sunday of the Year
Nb 11:25-29; Jm 5:1-6; Mk 9:38-43, 45, 47-48

Scandal

1. Scandal defined

The word "scandal" recurs in our newspapers, often enough making the headlines. The word is taken from the Latin *scandalum,* which means block or offense, in the sense of a stumbling-block. Its use in theology designates anyone or anything that's an occasion of sin. A scandal causes one to fall. Scandal obstructs growth or progress in holiness.

At one time God himself was considered by the ancient Hebrews to be an obstacle. They predicated the name "Rock" of him in a double sense. The first sense was favorable to him. He was to them as faithful and secure as a rock, the stone of strength. But, in an unfavorable sense, they also took him to be rock to trip over and fall, a rock of scandal. Whenever he displeased them, whenever he left them to their own undoing, he appeared to scandalize them.

Jesus too seemed at times, by his association with sinners, to be a stumbling-block or scandal to his countrymen. The Church gains the same reputation through her faults and sins, and for espousing causes contrary to current secular trends and upholding unpopular moral principles.

2. Scandal, more or less

Scandal, as applicable to God, Jesus, and the Church, may be a misnomer. People take offense too easily at the three from their own weak positions. Shocked at what they see wrong, they may be looking with jaundiced eye at things God, Jesus, and his Church do.

Just as some people are scandalized too easily, so others should take more shock at the sin, corruption, and crime that abound. Serious scandal exists wherever God is mocked, his laws flouted, and "where men are treated as mere tools for profit" (*Constitution on the Church in the Modern World, #27*).

Particularly disturbing and distasteful is the sight of adults who should know better, taking advantage of children and youth. Children and youth, at a tender and impressionable age, are utterly at the mercy of their elders. We can't imagine their potential for evil and the pressure of temptation upon them. The kind of corruption adults expose them to goes by the theological name of *diabolical* scandal. They enrich themselves at the moral expense of the innocent.

More precisely, the dope-peddlers, the sexual miscreants, homosexual and heterosexual, the sellers of pornography and obscenity—all fall under the category of scandal. "They poison human society, but they do more harm to those who practice them than those who suffer from the injury" (*idem*).

St. James in his letter denounces the unjust rich whose luxury and extravagance are scandalous. He has in mind the "exploitation of helpless poor masses by unscrupulous rich in the ancient world," but he might have written his letter for our times. This part of his letter is a warning to the rich and a mild consolation to the poor. He accuses the rich of a heartless injustice. They hoard their wealth rather than distribute it to the poor laborers by way of unpaid or insufficiently paid labor. Because they batten themselves on injustices to the laborer, decay and destruction will show them the emptiness of their wealth.

3. Bad example

Scandal, however, has lesser proportions. All of us are guilty of it inasfar as we give bad example. How socially culpable are we for the corrupt consequences of our conduct. Do we confess the bad example which is a stumbling-block to others? What about the neglect and abuse of children, the angry tantrums and foul language in their presence? Is it just to accuse others of their scandal and absolve ourselves of ours?

The charge of scandal is against us for whom the hand, foot, or eye is an occasion of sin. Instead of using the hand, foot, and eye, in other words, our whole selves, as potential for good we use them as potential for evil. The hand suggests the ability and capability of lending a helping hand to others. The foot takes us wherever we can do good. The eye opens upon a world in need of our love and sacrifice.

4. Resistance to scandal

The Old and New Testament readings suggest ways of resistance to scandal. We can renounce the evils to which the hand, foot, and eye bring us. Renunciation is a way of fighting off scandal. It may mean giving up drink, dope, sex, dishonesty, bad companionship, evil accomplices. The saints knew better than to attack some evils directly, which were too attractive for a frontal attack. The remedy against some scandal is as simple as that—run away from it.

The most effective way of overcoming the influence of evil is by the influence of good. The lusher the grass, the less danger there is of weeds cropping through it. The forces of evil are so strong that we need all the help we can get to combat them. We Catholic Christians have no monopoly on the goodness of God. We should welcome all assistance of justice, goodness, and truth. Such was the mind of Vatican II speaking for the Church: "The Council, therefore, looks with great respect upon all the true, good,

and just elements found in the very wide variety of insti-
tutions which the human race has established for itself and
constantly continues to establish" (*idem,* #42).

Moses didn't prohibit the seventy elders from acting
and speaking in God's name, on his authority; he only
wished there were more of them. Moses didn't see the elders as rivals to himself.

Nor did Christ object to non-Christians casting out
devils in his name.

Divine power can't be fenced in by space and time and
persons. God bestows his power to whom and when and
where he pleases. With his power we resist scandal and
perform extraordinary good deeds.

Twenty-seventh Sunday of the Year
Gn 2:9-11; Heb 2:9-11; Mk 10:2-16

Christian Marriage

1. Families in trouble

Our culture, in several respects, especially that of divorce, is becoming increasingly conspiratorial against the family. Therefore, this homily is meant to sound like a warning to family members. The question the Pharisees put to Christ about divorce was loaded. The challenge to family life today is no less threatening.

Here are several sample reports about the American family. The first is the leading statement in an article that appeared in a popular weekly news magazine. "American families are in trouble—trouble so deep and pervasive as to threaten the future of our nation." The most obvious sign of the trouble is divorce. Americans are divorcing each other almost enthusiastically at the rate of 80 divorces per hour. At least one in every four U.S. marriages ends in divorce.

The rise of the divorce rate is matched by the decline of the birth rate. The child is no longer a source of unity in the family. The birth rate has reached the point of zero population growth.

Second sample: A popular opinion poll asked a cross-section of Americans for agreement or disagreement upon this touchy statement: "The institution of marriage and the family as we have known it is becoming outmoded." About fifty percent, young and old, answered yes.

To protect the stability of marriage, marriage counseling agencies are mushrooming all over the country. But one counselor, styling himself humanist and in parenthesis "nondenominational, nonsectarian, and nontheistic," advocates instant matrimony, in sixty seconds flat, in his home. As counselor he would ask: "Do you marry each other?" Bride replies: "Yes." Groom: "Yes." Counselor adds: "I pronounce you man and wife. Good luck, you may need it."

The easiness of marriage should be paralleled with the easiness of divorce. One editorial writer proposes a non-fault divorce which would make for equality. He reasons from no-fault car insurance to no-fault divorce.

2. Man over animal

Within this contemporary cultural context with all its inconsistencies, let us try to understand the first and third scriptural readings. Take Genesis first, in its teaching about animals and the first family of man, and then combine it with Mark and his description of two situations involving divorce and children.

The Hebrews took primitive man's act of naming the animals as symbolizing his power, control over, and ownership of them. Man is so superior to animals that they can't or shouldn't be dignified with human rights and privileges.

It seems incongruous for a society to overpopulate pet and household animals and underpopulate children, but this is happening. Need man who seeks companionship turn to animals for it? In a friendless society must he rely upon animals for protection against his fellowman?

Genesis makes it very clear that animals can't replace man for companionship and friendship. After creating the animal world, God seeks a complement to the first man in the first woman. "It is not good that the man should be alone. I will make him a helpmate." He then fashions Eve in the same nature as Adam. Together, Adam and Eve, or man and woman, form the most intimate of human relationships—"they become one body."

3. One body in Christ

The intimacy of this relationship is compared to that of "one body." God exalted their union by comparing it to his faithful relationship to his people, or, preferably, to the membership we all have in the body of Christ. St. Paul sets up for the ideal of marriage the union of all men in Christ and discountenances the sin of fornication for being a false imitation of marital intercourse. He says further: "As you know, a man who goes with a prostitute is one body with her, since the two, as it is said, become one flesh. But anyone who is joined to the Lord is one spirit with him" (1 Cor 6:16).

4. Reasons against divorce

The ultimate reason against divorce is that it betrays the indissoluble relationship between God and his people, between Christ and his body, the Church. The practical reason, of course, is that in a divorce children are left without their rightful parents and consequently suffer the most. But even this reason is dependent on the indissoluble bond God has with his children, and Christ with his brothers. "So then, what God has united, man must not divide."

The Mosaic law, like our civil law, allowed for divorce. At the time Christ tangled with the Pharisees over divorce, two interpretations of divorce were in vogue. The one allowed divorce for adultery only; the other for any trivial reason—a cold dinner, a more attractive woman. Christ went against this trend by imposing a stricter interpretation than the Mosaic law. His action gives us pause to think: in the gradual breakdown of family life should we be relaxing divorce laws or tightening them?

Oddly enough, Jesus' meeting with the children is reported by Mark immediately after the debate with the Pharisees over divorce. The coincidence here may be entirely accidental. Jesus didn't want the children to be separated from himself any more than he wanted them separated from their parents.

No family is an island. It needs our support. We can be proud of the solid, wholesome and holy Christian families that will determine the future of our nation. Every family member has the same need as did the late Robert F. Kennedy: "His own relationship with his brothers and sisters and his parents were a source of strength and meaning. . . His character was formed in the crucible of family relationships. . ."

Twenty-eighth Sunday of the Year
Ws 7:7-11; Heb 4:12-13; Mk 10:17-30

Success in Life

Imagine yourself in the middle of this four-way conversation going on in the eternal now, which means today:

Solomon: You see, I was praying to the Lord for this gift of wisdom when it came to me. The funny thing was, I was willing to forsake everything I had—wealth, health, power, beauty, sunlight itself—in exchange for it, but I kept it all and had wisdom to boot. When I showed it to the Queen of Sheba, it made her head reel.

The young Dives: You couldn't have had it very long. What happened?

Solomon: You wouldn't believe it. I should have had more sense. It was all God's favor. Rather than put it all to his service, I squandered it. I blew it.

Dives junior: Impossible. With that wisdom, you would have known better.

Solomon: That's what you think. God-given wisdom didn't make me worldly-wise. Wisdom, plus the wealth and all, brought me into conflict. An old Greek philosopher once said that they are to be called wise who order things rightly and govern well. I had the reputation for wise government—for a while, but then my possessions and ambition twisted my thinking and ultimately upset me.

Dives junior: What's wrong with wealth? What's so dangerous about the good things of life?

Solomon: Nothing in themselves. I really enjoyed them. We Hebrews used to consider them signs of a divine blessing.

Dives junior: There you are. Take myself. I have enough wealth and prosperity to make me happy. I inherited it. I didn't come by it dishonestly, by defrauding or robbing the poor.

Solomon: That's not the point. I grant you it may be the case for some. But the danger of wealth and prosperity, at least for me, was that they tempted me to be self-sufficient. They made me forget my goal in life. The good things of life seem to have boundless depth, width, and height. I failed to see beyond their superficiality. They constitute no check list for success in life. Attach too much value to them, and they make life purposeless. Life has only one purpose—God. Everything else is superficial, in a sense "godless."

Dives junior: I felt some of that emptiness too. That's why I asked for eternal life, how to achieve that.

Peter: You two guys are out of my class. I had a little fishing line of business, not much, just enough to make a living. I gave it up.

Dives junior: You gave it up? But why?

Peter: Because of a mysterious summons from the Master. He came along one day as I was tending my nets and recruited me.

Dives junior: You abandoned one career to pursue another? That's a pretty big step to take, especially if you don't know what you're getting into.

Peter: I didn't have much to lose, you know. This Man had a fascinating power about him. I took the risk of joining him.

Solomon: What did he have to offer?

Peter: Not much either—in the way you may be thinking. For leaving everything behind, he promised payment a hundred times over. How about that?

Dives junior: Then what? Did he deliver on his promise?

Peter: Well, my luck with him was far better than at fishing. I was the happier for the change in my career. He shaped my life. He turned me into a full-fledged Christian,

showed me that one career should predominate and prevail in my life. And he spoke about a "world to come"
which would offer something you were looking for—
eternal life.

(At this moment the Man called the Master appears
on the scene.)

Solomon: We were just talking about you.

Peter: These two were discussing the relative merits
of wealth, its inflation, and I in my bungling way began to
devaluate it. By implication I was arguing for a spirit of
renunciation.

Jesus: Not bad. It would be a good thing if men would
periodically revalue the good things of life.

Solomon: We called it the wiser thing to do.

Jesus: May I quote to you from Vatican II's *Pastoral
Constitution on the Church in the Modern World?* Section
15 reads in part: "The intellectual nature of the human
person is perfected by wisdom and needs to be. For wisdom gently attracts the mind of man to a quest and a love
for what is true and good. Steeped in wisdom, man passes
through visible realities to those which are unseen." I go
along with that.

Dives junior: Sounds easy.

Peter: Not on your life. I can verify that—it's hard.

Jesus: I have to agree with Peter. This teaching has
penetrating power. It cuts through where the soul of man
is divided from his spirit, between the bone and its marrow.

Solomon: Are you saying it's impossible for the ordinary man?

Jesus: I'm saying how hard it is to enter the kingdom
of God. And it's double hard for one weighted down with
wealth. He has too much to carry . . . he should shed his
burden.

Dives junior: Then salvation is impossible for man?

Jesus: That's right. For man it's impossible, but not for
God. (He heads off.)

8

Twenty-ninth Sunday of the Year
Is 53:10-11; Heb 4:14-16; Mk 10:35-45

Trial and Triumph

1. The cup

James and John request a favor from their Master which isn't his to grant. The Matthean narration of the incident has their mother asking the favor for them. Her intercession helps them to look better, not so self-interested and pushy. The request seems very much like a political favor—choice spots in his kingdom. Then ten other apostles resent their squeeze play.

The Master puts them down not too gently. They really don't know what they're asking for. They don't know why they should be deserving of places in his kingdom of glory. Jesus lays down two conditions. The one is a cup, the other a baptism. By "cup" he means a destiny coinciding with his. His baptism is a suffering and death in cold blood. He promises them a trial, but not the kind of triumph they want.

2. What is temptation?

We don't ordinarily associate the idea of temptation with this incident, yet that's what it is. James and John aren't alone in being tempted to seek promotions. The temptation to superiority, to grandeur, to first-ranking positions attacks everybody. The easier way to think of temptation is in terms of *occasion* of sin—whatever offers sex, power, wealth, popularity. A more fundamental temptation undermines human life, a temptation in which life itself is a trial or test run.

The Lord allows the test to run the course of an entire

life, from beginning to end. Here and there during a lifetime one may fail a test, succumb to temptation, but that
isn't the whole of it. The biggest temptation is to waste
a life. The most Godforsaken life is one without any testing. It was said of King Hezekiah that "God only deserted
him to test him, and to discover the secrets of his heart"
(2 Ch 32:31). A human life put to a test reveals the secrets
of the heart. The choice open to the heart is a "Yes" or "No"
to its true destiny.

The form this test or trial takes is twofold. Call the
one temptation by desire, the other temptation by suffering. In fairness to them, we must say James and John were
tempted by the right kind of desire. Their failure was to
ask too much—box seats in the heavenly gallery.

3. Temptation by desire and suffering.

The temptation by desire most of us experience is not
to be content with an apprenticeship. We want to go the
whole hog, to be served rather than to serve. Our severest
trial is to try to pin God down, have him do our will, force
his hand. Patience toward God is a rare virtue. We must
learn to wait upon him, let him take his time, do his will,
allow him to come and go in our life as he pleases. When
we don't get our way, we fail, we break our great resolu-
tions repeatedly. "Human living is being-challenged-in-
the-world, not simply being-in-the-world," wrote Abraham
Heschel (*Who is Man?*, p. 105).

Temptation by suffering is the stuff that makes saints.
Name any saint you like, and upon examination of his or
her life you'll find the test of suffering.

Their secret of sanctity, however, isn't the suffering
itself. They succeed at turning it into a means of salvation
for others. The Savior spent "a life in atonement," and so
do they. "By his sufferings shall my servant justify many,
taking their faults on himself." In the same way the saints
serve their fellowmen.

4. Help from Christ

In neither case, the temptation by desire or the temptation by suffering, is the test too severe. Man can endure a lot, but he has his breaking-point. To keep him struggling, resisting temptation, refusing to admit defeat, he needs outside help. That help is assured in the grace of Christ. "The man who thinks he is safe must be careful that he does not fall. The trials that you have had to bear are no more than people normally have. You can trust God not to let you be tried beyond your strength, and with any trial he will give you a way out of it and the strength to bear it" (1 Cor 10:12f.).

The difference between triumph and defeat in trial is due to Jesus alone, and not to human power or strength. Over a lifetime of trial and suffering, nobody can stand it or go it alone. Jesus wasn't one "incapable of feeling our weaknesses with us." We have in him "One who has been tempted in every way that we are, though he is without sin." He not only had the same trials but he felt the need of companionship. He acknowledged this to his apostles: "You are the men who have stood by me faithfully in my trials."

The companionship the Master asked of James and John he demands of all his followers. A unique and mutual companionship, it puts Jesus into the very life of temptation we sustain. "Because he has himself been through temptation he is able to help others who are tempted" (Heb 2:18). His help is unlike that we give others in their hour of need. We might welcome sinners back into the Church, we might try to console somebody bedridden, we might carry foodstuffs or clothing to a needy neighbor, we might volunteer our aid in hospitals and care centers; all this, and more besides, is truly a Christian service. Nevertheless, it can't compare with Christ's companionship in trial and suffering. He's tempted *within us.*

5. Sharing the triumph

Once the struggle of life is over, Christ accompanies us in whatever triumph we achieve. He makes no promise that the temptation to greatness will ever leave us; he only guarantees it won't win out. The triumph is more certain than the trial. An English mystic, Mother Julian of Norwich, described her own trial and triumph this way: "God has not told me I shall not be tempested, or travailed or afflicted; he has promised only that I shall not be overcome." Triumph without trial would be an empty victory.

Thirtieth Sunday of the Year
Jr 31:7-9; Heb 5:1-6; Mk 10:46-52

Priest Forever

1. Vocations

Within the past year, three university students of my acquaintance switched careers, deciding to study for the priesthood. The first, a post-graduate student, gave up a teaching career. The second came to his decision after a freshman year of study on campus because, as he said, "I wanted to test out my vocation." The third, a teacher and married man with three children, after discussing his vocation with his wife, felt he should pursue studies for the priesthood of the Antiochian Orthodox Christian Church, to which they belonged.

That the three are becoming priests is admirable, and that they opted for that vocation in a difficult time of the priesthood is much more admirable. The priesthood today is caught in a whirlwind of low opinion, a so-called identity crisis. What should a priest be? His way of life? His work?

2. Causes of decline

Whatever the external causes for this decline, three factors, I think, are militating against the priesthood from within. The first is the question of a married clergy. As long as the debate over this is rife, it leaves the priesthood with a feeling of uncertainty. This question is compounded with the question of women priests. Is it likely that women priests will marry men priests? Last but not least is the number of priests leaving. All sorts of reasons are given for their departures: they want to marry, the Church is irrelevant, bogged down by rules and regulations, they find it hard to communicate with parishioners, the parishioners lack interest and devotion.

3. The priest

It comes as a peaceful lull in a raging storm—this letter to the Hebrews with its definition of the priesthood of Christ. It outlines the origin of the priest, his purpose, his powers, and his condition.

A priest is called by God, "taken out of mankind," out of family background, neighborhood, parish, seminary. No one is born into the priesthood; a development toward the priesthood does take place within the family and Church. A young or old man responds to the divine call personally and voluntarily. That response lasts through his years of learning and formation and through his priestly life.

His sole purpose is to render, for the sake of Christ, the great high priest, religious service to his people, "to act for men in their relations with God." In detailing this priestly service the letter to the Hebrews is a bit narrow. It limits the priest to ministry at the altar, namely, to offering sacrifice. This is his principal function, but he has others too, for his priesthood is cast in the mold of the Old Testament where a specialized, professional priesthood developed which gave all its time and labor to the ministry.

4. Man of prayer, teacher

The priest is a man of prayer. Therefore, for his own spirituality and for that of his people he regularly confers with God. Through prayer he learns the divine will and proclaims it to men.

Study enables the priest to be the teacher of that divine law which encompasses man's entire duty before God. "The lips of the priest ought to safeguard knowledge; his

mouth is where instruction should be sought, since he is
the messenger of Yahweh Sabaoth" (Ml 2:7). More time
and effort are required of the priest in a changeover such
as the church is experiencing. Continuing education is a
must for the priest. Who would be so foolish as to entrust
his health to a quack doctor or outmoded medical practi-
tioner? If health is that precious, how much more so is
our spiritual welfare.

The priesthood today is an outgrowth of several roles
and special functions dating back to both Old and New
Testament times. The priesthood of Christ is traced back
to the order of Melchizedek. Our priesthood derives from
his and from other historical antecedents—the disciples,
apostles, presbyter-bishops, Eucharistic celebrants. All
priestly functions are like spans of a bridge between God
and man. Unless the priest gets your support, his bridge-
building leads to nowhere.

5. No apology

My holding up this mirror to the present-day priesthood isn't motivated by self-pity or by desire for glory or
by criticism of the priests who have left. The mirror, I
hope, isn't falsifying the reality. The priest "can sympa-
thize with those who are ignorant or uncertain because
he too lives in the limitations of weakness."

The priesthood is itself an honor and dignity, hence it
needs no empty glorification or false advertising. When
we admit to a clergy crisis, a loss of confidence in priests,
and catch sight of the dirty wash of the priesthood, it's
impossible to close our eyes and be blind to the situation.
Let us face it together.

6. Moral and spiritual leadership

Better days aren't ahead for faith and religion till moral
and spiritual leadership are restored. A change for the

better in the priesthood will renew the Church. Reflect upon your own home. What sort of reputation does the clergy have in it? How do you speak about priests? If the religious spirit is at a low ebb in your home, you might consider that question. Undue criticism of the clergy breaks down the religious spirit. Christ remarked about a group of moral and spiritual leaders in his day: "They are blind men leading blind men; and if one blind man leads another, both will fall into a pit" (Mt 15:14).

The crowds tried to hush up the blind man who shouted to Christ for a cure. Christ cured him and sent him off: "Go, your faith has saved you." That same faith will save the Church in its need for moral and spiritual leadership. Faith is a receptivity to God's healing word and a confident self-abandonment to God whose saving power is exercised in and through Christ. Faith in what? In the power Jesus has and has bestowed on his priests.

Solemnity of All Saints
Rv 7:2-4, 9-14; 1 Jn 3:1-3; Mt 5:1-12

Saints in Our Future

1. The happy life

The practice of the faith has much to recommend itself —a happy life. We have a glorious future ahead, provided we move into it. No walk of life can make the same claim or guarantee as the Christian way of life. This is no sales pitch for faith or religion but a fact of life. Then why, do you suppose, aren't people beating a path to the churches, shouting for joy, and crowding the gates of heaven? The reason is simple.

The happy life the Lord of heaven and earth offers prescribes necessary qualifications. People aren't jauntily journeying heavenward instead of hellward minus the necessary qualifications. They need—to speak in the language of biblical poetry—to be dressed in the white robe of a life of virtue, holding the palm branch of victory in their hands. In other words, the steps leading to the happy life are the good works they perform along the way of life. And they attain their goal of victory through Christ. He gains the triumph for them and in them.

Still one can press the question—why? Why the necessary qualifications for man, weak and corrupt? Would God be more merciful to save man without making him qualify? God, with no loss to himself, could write off the debt of man's sin.

Such questions indicate a forgetfulness of what the happy life is: a gift from God. He can and does state his own terms. Not for any selfish reason, but the sake of his people. They would be most unhappy in a heavenly state for which they didn't qualify. Like birds in a cage, or fish out of water.

2. The will to sainthood

After all, the only requirement for heaven is holiness, and only God can clothe us with it, for he alone is holy. God the Father wants his children to be with him for eternity. We *are* God's children; "we shall be like him because we shall see him as he really is." The desire and the will to be holy are enough to start us out. "Always be wanting the holiness without which no one can ever see the Lord" (Heb 12:14). "Surely everyone who entertains this hope must purify himself, must try to be as pure as Christ," that is, as sinless as Christ. Sinlessness is beyond our capability, but a will out of sinfulness is a way.

What kind of saint do we need nowadays? A new type of saint, one suitable for our age. The new kind of saint holds himself responsible for the world, to transform it for God. The people he lives with will show him the work it takes to straighten out the world for God. He meets with daily demands. He doesn't go about wearing a button advertising his availability for sanctity. His work isn't brilliant or dazzling. The people who walk or work with him may note nothing special, though he does his job extremely well.

3. An outline

The eight beatitudes outline the success story of the saint. Even though the beatitudes draw bits of wisdom from the ages, they contemporize the life of a saint. Poor in spirit, the saint is one of the *anawim* who are dependent on divine mercy. Gentle, the opposite of rough and inconsiderate. Mournful over wrongdoing, hungry and thirsty for whatever is right. Toward those who offend merciful. His purity in heart befits him eventually for the sight of

God. As one called to be a saint, bound to suffer, persecuted. In each and every case, whether poor or oppressed,
his story has a happy ending.

The biblical outline of holiness, so brief but beautiful,
is enfleshed with the lives of the saints. The Lord leaves
us not with a bare outline, he fills in the blank spaces with
real live models of holiness. The saints whose names we
bear are excellent imitations of Christ, our guides, teach-
ers of how to live.

4. Calendar of saints

Their number overruns the symbolical 144,000; their
number is countless. They keep crowding themselves out
of the Church calendar. You may remember how, before
the revision of the Roman Missal in 1969, most of the liturgical calendar was taken up with the celebration of saints'
feasts. The anonymous saints are crowded up in one day,
all commemorated at once in a summary way.

Today, since life has become more business-like, more
legal, more commercial, more industrial, we need a day set
aside to honor the saints. Wherever we go we have need of
saints marvelously portraying the life of Christ in our
midst.

5. Our heroes

We elect the stars of baseball, football, hockey, and
others to halls of fame. The liturgy of All Saints is like a
visit to their hall of fame. On this roster of stars no names
appear equivalent to the George Herman "Babe" Ruth's
and Mildred "Babe" Didrikson's of the sports world. The
happy life they enjoy is held up to us for an ideal and goal.
If we could make them any happier, it would be by joining
their company. How much better company can we keep
than the fellowship of the saints?

By professing our faith in the communion of saints we

imply our need for their support. We do require their heroic example, their cheerful intercession in the happy life. The saints witness to what love can do and to that never-ending joy which flows from love. They are the happier now for not holding back when living on this earth. They gave no excuses for their faults; they sought no escape from their crosses; they didn't dodge their duties; they didn't slouch on the job of Christian living. Happy are they, and happy shall we be by becoming the saints of the future.

Thirty-first Sunday of the Year
Dt 6:2-6; Heb 7:23-28; Mk 12:28-34

Three-dimensional Love

1. Two in agreement

The gospel describes a rare occurrence: Jesus and the Scribe come to point of agreement, a point of law. To appreciate the agreement between the two, Jesus and Scribe, we must understand who the latter is. His first duty is to study and interpret the Scriptures, a man learned in the law, wisdom literature, and prophetical teaching. He studies oral tradition too, and is known for his rigorous interpretation of the law, at times for his vanity and hypocrisy.

Jesus is often at odds with the Scribes and Pharisees. When they agree, they arouse surprise and interest. One confrontation after another, instead of bringing them together in a meeting of minds, erects a wall of separation between them. The Scribes and Pharisees pull farther and farther apart from Jesus in their nit-picking interpretations of the law. They avoid the Gentiles, sinners, and Jews whom they consider below their standing, the very company Jesus seeks out for himself.

2. Two at odds

The present-day religious situation isn't much different. Oh, the ecumenical spirit is still in the air, while the various religions, eastern and western, differ on many points. On one point, however, which is the core or heart of religion, there can be no disagreement: ". . . you must love the Lord your God with all your heart, with all your soul, with all your mind and with all your strength . . . you must love your neighbor as yourself."

Jesus and the Scribe in their friendly discussion prefigure the ecumenical dialogues of today. Religion, seemingly always a controversial topic, can cause much rub and rancor. The Scribes and Pharisees in Jesus' time held that the commandments were of greater or lesser obligation. Jesus agreed. They also agreed upon the principle of righteous living taught in Deuteronomy 6:5 and Leviticus 19:18, the primary duty of man to love God and neighbor.

3. Love and the will of God

The nub of their dispute arose in the interpretation of the law. Scribes and Pharisees thought the love of neighbor should extend no further than their own kind. Jesus set no boundaries to neighborly love. He cut through the net of legalism entangling the Scribes and Pharisees and summarized the law into a twofold commandment. The Jews professed this in their prayer, morning, noon, and night. For this point of mutual understanding Jesus praised the Scribe.

They were in accord in accepting the will of God the Father. His will to love excludes no one, makes no distinction between friend and enemy. The basis of Jesus' commandment to love is nothing else than what God wills and does. God in Christ befriends the common people, fellow-travelers, and prostitutes; he loves the unloved and the loveless.

His teaching about love was somewhat modified by the early Church. Christians then believed their first obligation of love was to their own members. They upheld the universality of Christian love; they felt charity should begin at home; love at home should reach out to others, whatever their race, nationality, or creed.

4. Three-in-one love

The love Jesus commands is three-dimensional, triangular: God, my neighbor, and myself. Love of God is inseparable from love of neighbor and from love of oneself. Absence of the one dimension topples the other dimensions. Credit must be given to the Christians who deepened the meaning of all three—God, neighbor, love.

Too often we think of love as two-dimensional, a tit for tat relationship. We extend love only to the degree we receive it from God and from our neighbor. Is this Christian love?

God being but one, love of him has to be one love, undivided and unconditional. The depth of this love is plumbed in the heart, soul, mind, and strength. Man must love him with mind and will, namely, with his whole self, completely. Any reservations to this love sets limits to the infinity of divine love.

5. All-inclusive love

The love of neighbor is all-inclusive—any man in need, and every man is in need of love. The question, "Who is my neighbor?" resolves itself into, "To whom am I neighbor?" I am to be neighbor to anyone who requires my help. The very fact that someone needs help entitles him to be my neighbor. His need is his claim upon me, and I am unfree in the total family of God to disown him. God doesn't have to call me to his help by some sort of inspiration; his need is enough to sound the alarm for help. Am I ready to lend a helping hand? Thus the love of neighbor is the test of the love of God.

We are mostly in love with ourselves, in the desire of whatever is good for ourselves. The more conscious we are of this fact, the more we should know what we owe our neighbor, for our duty is to love him *as ourselves.* Locked up in ourselves, the commandment of love is the master key that unlocks us. The needy are heard knocking at the door. Once love has opened the door and let itself out, there can be no egotism left, no spare corner or closet for self-love.

The Scribe declared love of neighbor far more important than any holocaust or sacrifice. Jesus heard how wisely he spoke and commented how close he was to God's kingdom. Should the various religions forget their petty religious differences and concentrate upon the twofold summary of love, they would put a stop to many who question the value of religion today. The religious spirit would do little else but exemplify three-dimensional love to a world badly in need of it.

Thirty-second Sunday of the Year
1 K 17:10-16; Heb 9:24-28; Mk 12:38-44

A *Mite Selfless*

1. Studies in contrast

Scribe and Scribes are studies in contrast. Last Sunday's Scribe is praised for his summarizing the Mosaic law in love of God and neighbor. This Sunday's Scribes are criticized for their pride and hypocrisy, their exacting heavy dues for the temple worship, and their scrupulous attention to little things, outward observances. They were great showmen.

Now, taking them as a lot, the Scribes and Pharisees contrast even more with the two widows we hear about. Among the Hebrews it was a disgrace to be a widow. Widows had no right of inheritance according to Hebrew law. It was for this reason, because they needed his help, that the Lord was called the "defender of widows" (Ps 28:5) and took care of them (Ps 146:9).

Out of a sense of justice if not of charity, the Scribes and Pharisees should have stood up for the widows. Instead, they treated them shamefully and exploited their gullibility and good will.

2. Two widows

At first sight, it looks as if the prophet Elijah imposed himself on the poor widow in the Old Testament story. He compelled her to share with him her last jar of meal and last jug of oil, the only things left between herself and starvation. As the story turned out, neither jar nor jug were spent or emptied. She was rewarded for her generosity.

Almost the same thing happens in the New Testament story of the widow worshipping in the temple. Others—the wealthy—support the temple with what they have extra, from their surplus. The poor widow gives the smallest donation, a mite, somewhat equivalent to a penny, her last possession. The quantity of her gift doesn't matter as much as its quality. What she donates represents her self, her life.

Imagine yourself in the situation of the two widows. How would you feel if you were asked to give away till it hurts? Suppose you saw your beneficiaries live more comfortably than you do. If they took advantage of you, poached on your possessions, would you still be willing to contribute? We have to place ourselves in their situation to realize what the widows were up against.

3. A bit of history

The financial support of the temple in the Old Testament came from the offerings of the people. The temple treasury was also filled with tax money. The priests and their helpers gained from the sacrifices offered in the temple and from the tithing. These were the four sources of temple income.

Since the ancient Hebrews were an agricultural people, they were asked to tithe on their land produce and cattle. The dues they paid were in terms of corn, wine, oil, herbs. In return for their payments they were promised prosperity. For non-payment they were threatened with a death penalty. Neither promise nor threat kept them from withholding their dues now and then.

The system of tithing varied from time to time according to historical circumstances. In New Testament times the Hebrews paid taxes to Rome amounting to twenty-five percent of their yield. How does that figure compared with the taxes you pay nowadays? Over and above the Roman tax they had to pay twenty-two percent of their remaining

income to the temple, and a second tithe to the poor.
Neither of the two were always paid. No wonder why.

It doesn't take much imagination to see, nor is it face-
tious or satirical to say, that in some agricultural designs
churches and banks are look-alikes. This fact goes far back
into history. The Jerusalem temple had a safety deposit
system for money and valuables. And it had its own police
force, the ancient counterpart to an electronic alarm
system.

4. A common complaint

I hear the complaint occasionally, and I rather think
you do even more often, that the Church is concerned too
much about money and preaches for it too frequently.
Pastors who shoulder the administration of the parish are
said to harp on the subject. Be that as it may, the Church
in her ministry can hardly do without financial support.

Christ himself appointed someone in his apostolic group
to carry the common purse. He advised his disciples that
"the labourer deserves his wages" (Lk 10:7). St. Paul, in
addition to working for his livelihood by tent-making, gave
the same advice.

5. Alternatives

The alternatives to the ecclesiastical collection of
money have been tried and proved no better. One of them
is to have a state-supported Church. Such money still
comes from the people of God. The only difference is that
it passes through the government hands and is designated
for church use. The entanglements with civil government
which Church history bears witness to, have shown themselves to be of no advantage to the Church.

Another alternative is to let the clergy be entirely self-
supporting. The argument in its favor is that then clergy-
men will experience firsthand how hard it is to make a

living. They will hesitate to solicit money and be less inclined to spend it foolishly. The argument sounds good; its big defect is that such a system leaves the Church with much less of a ministry. Can ministers of the altar then give themselves full-time to the desires and needs of their people?

The real question the cases of the widows put to us isn't the quantity of our giving to the Church but the quality. The humblest and quietest givers are the people most acceptable to Christ, like the widows who contribute to Church support with the mind and intention of self-sacrifice. What they donate comes from the heart. They give of their very selves.

Thirty-third Sunday of the Year
Dn 12:1-3; Heb 10:11-14, 18; Mk 13:24-32

Great Distress

1. Providing for the future

This isn't the season for inventory in the business world, but it is, if it may be called such, in the liturgical year. It can be seen from the readings today, all of which refer to the last times and the age to come. This is the season to take stock of ourselves, to see whether our lives are directed toward everlasting life or everlasting disgrace. With no time to waste, the option isn't something we can put off.

Suppose we feel ourselves quite well prepared for the end of our days, ready to meet our judge. Will we be like the senior citizens who prepared themselves for their retirement? They looked ahead, scraped and saved for the future, thinking their earnings would provide them with some security, a peaceful and happy retirement. Then, to their utter distress and embarrassment, the inflated economy or other misfortunes destroyed all their hopes. Their savings gradually disappeared. Will we be caught in the same fix when judgment day comes?

The senior citizens are hardly to blame for their feelings of disappointment. Others will undergo the same sad experience who place their hopes in a totally man-made future. We should blame those who offer a program of human salvation.

2. Two ideologies

Two ideologies still trying to capture the hearts of men are communism and capitalism. Both tempt man with a rosy vision of the future. Both claim to be looking out for the welfare of mankind. But both explain everything in material terms. Both want to play God.

When you boil their teachings down to a few basic and fairly simple ideas, communism and capitalism are not much different. Both hold to some degree that work and production make history, and in making history they make man. Man can master himself and nature through his work. He can plan and build his own future universe. Given enough time and work, he'll construct a world of progress, freedom, and peace.

As our senior citizens found out already, and as we ourselves are finding out through disillusionment with them, the two ideologies falsify the picture of man and the world. Politics and economics are unable to reform and renew the world. Man, in order to achieve any real progress, to move upward in his history, can't be pushed from below by material factors. He can only be pulled from above by God. Man's *self*-perfection is made possible by God the source of salvation.

With eyes open to the course of history and contemporary events, we ought to see the falsity of the communistic and capitalistic philosophies of life. Communists hold out the hope of an ideal human community, capitalists substitute the idea of progress for the end of the world. Their calculations about the future of mankind are poor alternatives to Christian beliefs in a life to come.

3. The Bible and the future

Christianity has limited this-worldly concerns but unending other-worldly goals. It makes no promises for the future it can't keep. The language the Bible uses to predict the future of man and the world is apocalyptic. This reveals less about the future than it warns about the present. The future, it says, is a key to the present. The future, however, stores up no pot of gold at the end of the rainbow (as communists predict), nor a myth of progress (as capitalists promise).

In describing the future the Bible employs figurative language for two reasons. Its use of a kind of code language prevents harm to the Christians in the days of persecution. And it has to substitute for a better insight into the future. Samplings of this language are found in the readings today. The angel Michael warns and protects the friends of God. The budding fig tree is a sign of the impending end of the world. Sun and moon (once worshipped as gods) will fail to give their light. The world will collapse like a huge balloon.

Apocalyptic writing, which flourished two centuries before Christ and two after, doesn't paint the immediate future in glowing colors. Rather, it calls attention to the end of time, "that time of distress," "a time of great distress." The apocalyptic writer tussles with the question: why do some people, sometimes the most undeserving, get all the breaks in life? A main purpose in his writing is to proclaim a day of judgment when the answer to this question will be clearly seen, everyone will get his due, and a new world will supplant the old. Apocalyptic writing sounds direful at first, then has a happy ending.

4. The Lord of history

More important than the destiny of man is the role of God in the end-time. History may seem to be out of joint now, and God helpless and powerless to defend the innocent. But a final struggle will ensue between God and the powers of evil, in which he will show who is master. However much men may foul up his providence, God will prove himself the Lord of history. Christ turned his life into "one single offering," "one single sacrifice for sins." So God will follow up the time of distress with a single and final victory.

If we expect some telltale signs of the end, a pattern

or series of events that will tip us off early enough to put our earthly affairs in order, we can't be more mistaken. Too many would-be prophets have been wrong in foretelling the end of the world. The kingdom of God is working itself out in history mysteriously.

This apocalyptic description isn't to be taken literally then. After a time of distress which we all feel in a lifetime, a fulfillment of our hope will dawn. We're encouraged to regard human history from a religious point of view. Then we can see the Son of Man coming in glory, with the judgment, resurrection and life everlasting following him.

Solemnity of Christ the King
Dn 7:13-14; Rv 1:5-8; Jn 18:33-37

King of Kings

1. King and kingdom

For a minor theme in the funeral liturgy the Church directs our thoughts to the eternal reign of Christ the King. At the end of a human life, when the sight of death makes us feel so helpless, so much in the hands of God, the Church fittingly hails "the Lord Jesus Christ, king of endless glory." When death severs all human ties, the Church prays, "Lord, make us one in your kingdom."

The fact of Christ and his kingdom comprise the theme of this solemnity, marking the end of the liturgical year. As the old year dies out and the new begins, the Church in apocalyptic language sketches her eschatological doctrine of the end of the world and its restoration. Apocalyptic is a "bridge" spanning the Old Testament and the New, linking the prophets with Christ.

2. Apocalyptic

The prophetical book of Daniel does this very thing. Written about 167-164 B.C., at the start of the apocalyptic movement, it depicts the rise and fall of empires and the prospect of a kingdom to last forever. Jesus finds this apocalyptic convenient in explaining his own kingdom to his followers. Jesus and the early Christians keep a lively interest in apocalyptic. Later ages, for reasons of their own, lost interest in it, and only in more recent times has apocalyptic been restudied.

One feature of apocalyptic writing, though, has little

or no appeal: the idea of kingdom. We may welcome kings and queens to our country, regard them with some awe and regale them, but kingship itself is remote from our culture.

3. No earthly ruler

The ancient Hebrews lived in a kingdom till the year 587 B.C., the time of the exile. They never held their kings to be divine, as other ancient people did (Egyptians, Babylonians, Greeks, Romans). The thought and inspiration of kingship nonetheless persisted and kept their hope alive for a king who would liberate them from foreign oppression. They were wrong in this expectation, and so are we in expecting Christ's Church to intervene politically in world or national affairs.

So, with all due respect for royalty, does it really matter whether the Hebrews or we have had so little experience of kingship? We might have a purer and more realistic expectation of our King by not confusing him with earthly kings and rulers. He emphatically said his Kingdom was not of this world: "But my kingdom is not of this kind"— not of the kind that needs a national spirit, political machinery, or military defense.

4. The kingdom within

Where then do we find traces of Christ's kingdom, just where does it exist in the here and now? Or is "Christ the King" only a honorofic title? No, Christ reigns in the hearts and minds of men. His is a kingdom of love, light, peace. He rules where truth and rest prevail. People belong to his kingdom who experience "a new life."

Some proofs have already been shown of his real kingdom. First of all it has become manifest in Christ himself. That he overcame death by his resurrection was evidenced by his appearances to his disciples, to reassure

them, and by the empty tomb. His resurrection established
the fact that he is king of creation, that life and death are
in his power.

More up-to-date evidence of his kingdom is discoverable in his Church. Admittedly, the Church doesn't yet
overlap with his kingdom, but by love and service to mankind it is advancing toward the day of completion. Every
act of love and sacrifice adds to the kingdom. In perform-
ing good deeds for your neighbor think of yourselves as
builders of his kingdom.

5. The final stage

The final stage of Christ's kingdom is yet to come.
World powers come and go, but the kingdom of God will
be everlasting. They try with every means of human power
to put an end to oppression, crime, pain, and death. The
end of all evil is possible to the Son of Man alone, *the* man,
the *essential* man without whom humanity would ultimately fail and destroy itself. The Son of Man is one who
upsets and revises so many materialistic and secularistic
values. He has the power to recreate the values that will
endure forever, the values that neither moths can eat away
nor thieves can break into and steal, the values that make
us truly human.

Christ is king, "the Ruler of the kings of the earth,"
though he has no aspirations for an early kingdom. Earthly
kings and rulers—we should count ourselves among them
to the extent we want to rule our own lives—resist him and
his kingdom (see Pss 2,72). Whenever we set ourselves
up in opposition to him we imply, "We will not have this
man rule over us." The showdown of strength between
him and earthly rulers will come at the final age of the
world.

What we believe about Christ the King and his kingdom will be *realized* and *seen* fully at the great and last
judgment of the world. Christ the triumphant king will

return in the role of a judge (Dn 7:13). We may wonder sometimes why anarchy, tyranny, imperialism, and militarism seem to hold sway in the world. Will all such injustice ever receive its due punishment? Yes, for if we think kings and rulers thwart God's purposes we need only recall the kingships of Nebuchadnezzar and Cyrus who played into God's hands .

All of us who serve Christ the King will, because elevated to "a line of kings . . . to serve our God and to rule the world" (Rv 5:10), share in the judgmentary role. "They shall judge nations, rule over peoples, and the Lord will be their King forever" (Ws 3:8).